LEARNING ON THE RUN

Learning on the Run

ACTIVE CHRISTIAN LEARNING EXPERIENCES FOR TEENAGERS AND ADULTS

TED ENDACOTT

Scripture Union

Learning on the run
Copyright © 1992 Ted Endacott

All rights reserved. No portion of this publication may be reproduced in any form or by any means without prior permission of the publisher, with exception of pages from the thirty-five activities in chapters one to seven, which purchasers may copy for immediate and limited use in the context of their work with young people and adults.

Scripture Union books are published by
ANZEA PUBLISHERS
3-5 Richmond Road,
Homebush West NSW 2140 Australia.

ISBN 0-85892-468-4

Cover art and book design by Richard Knight
Typeset by A K Graphics Pty. Ltd. Bundeena NSW
Illustrations by the author
Printed in Singapore by Singapore National Printers

CONTENTS

Learning on the run	**7**
Acknowledgments	**8**
How this book works	**9**
Guide to activities in this book	**10**
Chapter one: Wide games	**12**
Chapter two: Simulation games	**30**
Laws of Christian education I	**46**
Chapter three: Role-plays	**47**
Chapter four: Enacted Bible readings	**62**
Laws of Christian education II	**80**
Chapter five: Drama	**81**
Chapter six: Board games	**99**
Laws of Christian education III	**118**
Chapter seven: Values clarification activities	**119**

LEARNING ON THE RUN

This is an approach to *Christian learning* that encourages participants, whether **KIDS** or **ADULTS,** to *discover things* for **THEMSELVES.** The emphasis is on **ACTION** and **INVOLVEMENT,** so a lot of *movement,* **NOISE,** *emotion* and *hard thinking* goes on. It can be argued that **JESUS** *often taught* in this style. *Academics* call it a **'PRAXIS' STYLE** (that means 'action' in Greek) as it involves a *cycle of* **ACTION** *followed by* **REFLECTION.** That cycle makes for *enjoyable, memorable* and **EFFECTIVE** learning.

ACKNOWLEDGMENTS

I am grateful to:

Three organisations which have helped me to grow in this area of education. The world wide scouting movement has nurtured wide-gaming for many decades. Pioneer camps in Alberta, Canada showed me how to mix simulations and wide-games. Scripture Union, Victoria, tolerated ten years of experimentation as I created and tested the methods in this book.

Three enthusiastic friends from Scripture Union who helped create a number of the activities in this book. Laurie Barton worked with me on the staff, while Peter Tindale and Brian Crisp were senior voluntary camp workers.

Three patient supporters on the home front. They allowed me to spend countless hours apping away at a word processor. To my wife Anita, and to my children Eric and Melanie, I dedicate this book.

Ted Endacott
September 1992

How this book works

Each activity is set out as follows:

SYMBOLS
At the start of the activity is a set of symbols which tells you, at a glance, the following:

INDOOR ACTIVITY — OUTDOOR ACTIVITY — EITHER ACTIVITY — AGE GROUP — DURATION — No. OF PLAYERS

DESCRIPTION
A thumbnail sketch of the activity and its aims.

CHECKLIST
A brief list of items needed for the activity. The 'samples' section has examples of many of these.

PREPARATION
Helpful explanations and advice on how to get ready.

RUNNING THE ACTIVITY
This section shows, in timetable form, how the activity might run for a specified age group.

ESSENTIAL RULES
For players and organisers to remember.

SAMPLES
These vary but include examples of maps, suggested scoring systems, play scripts, problem cards, and questions and Bible passages for discussion. If these samples meet the needs of your group, use them as they are; if they don't suit, adapt them. It is usually easier to modify something than to start from scratch.

VARIATIONS
These may show how to simplify the activity, or add some surprising new twists.

CROSS REFERENCES
These link the activity to similar ones elsewhere in the book.

Initially you may prefer to follow the instructions as provided. As you become more confident, I hope that you will start to adapt and modify. The possibilities are endless. So be creative and full of adventure!

'Until we did the drama that night around the fire, I never really understood how to become a Christian.'. Excited teenager who had just been on his first camp.

'I didn't like it, 'cos it made me think' - A low-achieving teenager who normally 'turned off' when a study got underway. This time a values clarification activity fully involved her in deep discussions.

'If I'd known I was going to die, I wouldn't have worried so much about the money!'- a reflection from a middle-aged man who had just experienced the Death Angel simulation game.

'It made me realise how precious my Bible really is.' Young woman who had her Bible snatched by the secret police in the simulation '1984'.

'Get lost! this story doesn't come from the Bible!'- disbelieving youth who had participated in an enacted reading based on the King David and Bathsheba incident.

LEARNING ON THE RUN

WIDE GAMES

These are usually physically active games involving rival teams. Players roam through wide areas of rural or urban space (hence the name 'wide game'). and generally live out the role of a person in a different country, culture, or era. For this reason wide games require a lot of time to set up, and to discuss at the finish. Because players are so fully involved, the teaching points are remembered for a long time.

SIMULATION GAMES

Each game 'simulates' or copies a valuable experience, often one that most people would not normally have. These experiences can be exciting, even stressful, but they force players to think carefully about their faith, their values, and their behaviour. As in wide games, you need ample time for discussion at the end. The teaching points are hard to forget.

ROLE-PLAYS

Participants briefly act out a scene and imagine themselves 'in some- one else's shoes'. This activity helps them to identify with the joys and the pain of others, and is a safe way to prepare for a new role - e.g. street evangelism, counselling work, or conflict resolution. It is highly rated as a training tool.

The cheating game
Why do we live below God's standards?

10 - 25   3 - 4 hours   12 - 200

Death Angel
Life without God is pointless

10 - 100   1.5 - 2 hours   30 - 900

Faith sharing
How to give your faith away

10 - 100   1 - 2 hours   6 - 600

The Prophet of Truth
Is outreach important for the Church?

16 - 100   3 - 4 hours   16 - 200

Shipwrecked
Finding time to look at your life

12 - 60   4 - 24 hours   4 - 40

The blockage
Building apologetics skills

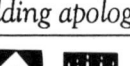 
12 - 100   1.5 - 2 hours   12 - 100

The great haggis hunt
The church needs teamwork to run well

10 - 100   6 - 24 hours   16 - 200

Sell it if you can
What is 'good' evangelism?

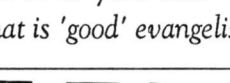

15 - 100   2 - 3 hours   40 - 120

Conflict at home
Child/parent tensions

10 - 50   1.5 - 2 hours   10 - 50

Life is not a picnic
Are we ready to show practical love?

10 - 100   2 - 3 hours   16 - 200

The politicians
The role isn't easy or simple

15 - 100   1.5 - 2 hours   15 - 50

Don't apologise
Confident evangelism

12 - 100   1.5 - 2 hours   10 - 100

Help for Slobovia
Fighting world poverty isn't easy!

14 - 30   4 - 24 hours   20 - 200

'1984'
Living in a persecuted church

16 - 30   2 - 3 hours   15 - 50

Church at war
How to make peace

10 - 100   1.5 - 2 hours   10 - 100

GUIDE TO ACTIVITIES IN THIS BOOK

ENACTED BIBLE READINGS

The main ingredient here is a passage from the Bible. A narrator reads it aloud and the participants mime, role-play or act out the events in the story. This can be a very simple process, or it may involve a sophisticated script and elaborate props.

DRAMA

In this book the term 'drama' covers scripted plays, narrated mimes and 'improvised' plays. These are short and ideal for beginners. People can grow enormously through putting on a simple performance. With drama you can say things you would never dare discuss.

BOARD GAMES

These typically involve a 'Monopoly' board and a pile of question cards. You can decide how personal, or how difficult, the questions are. Participants enjoy the challenge, and find the small-group environment stimulating.

VALUES CLARIFICATION ACTIVITIES

The name says it all. These activities encourage players to think through their values and beliefs. Having clarified their thinking, participants then compare their personal ethics with those of the Bible. This process can be used for evangelism or for discipleship training.

The Pearl
The parable of Matthew 13: 45-46

10 - 100   0.5 - 1 hour   10 - 100

The lifeboat
Explores responses to the gospel

15 - 100   15 mins   6 - 12

Saint of the century
General Bible knowledge

18 - 100   1-1.5 hours   8 - 80

Think for yourself
Reaction game involving forced choice

10 - 100   0.5 - 1 hour   10 - 1000

David and Bathsheba
The story from II Samuel

12 - 100   1 - 2 hours   10 - 100

What time is it?
Teaches awareness of others' needs

10 - 100   15 mins   6 - 12

Truth or dare
Encourages sharing of beliefs

13 - 21   1-1.5 hours   8 - 80

The starting point
Oxford debate showing spread of opinion

16 - 100   1 - 1.5 hours   12 - 1000

The disciples go out
The story from Luke 10:1-12

10 - 100   0.5 - 1 hour   10 - 100

Cross for sale
The cost of discipleship

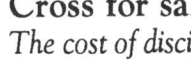
10 - 100   15 mins   2

Hot spot
Christian ethics for teenagers

11 - 18   0.5-1 hour   8 - 80

The hiding place
Moral dilemma stories

16 - 100   1 - 1.5 hours   10 - 100

The Exodus
The story from Exodus 1, 12, 14

8 - 100   1 - 1.5 hours   20 - 200

Ben David's store
God's rescue bid

10 - 100   0.5 - 2 hours   8 - 30

Boama Village
Applying the gospel to life

16 - 100   1 - 2 hours   8 - 80

The measuring machine
Grids for evaluating and assessing

16 - 100   0.5 - 1 hour   2 - 1000

The Lost Son
The parable of Luke 15: 1-32

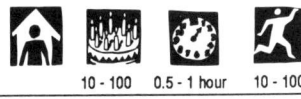
10 - 100   0.5 - 1 hour   10 - 100

Gratitude
Responses to God's love

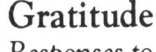
10 - 100   15 mins   8

Youth camp
Problem solving for youth leaders

18 - 40   1 - 1.5 hours   8 - 80

Heavy, heavy questions
Personal reflection exercises

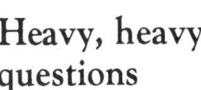
16 - 100   1-1.5 hours   2 - 1000

Chapter one
Wide games

What on earth is a 'wide game'?
To put it simply, it is an activity with all the purpose, rules and structures of a game. It is special because it must be played over a wide area, and involves considerable movement. A modest game might run for an hour on an oval, while a heroic version could range over kilometres of forest and last up to 24 hours. Players live out the role of a person in another country, culture, or time period e.g. a politician or a peasant. Note that the games in this chapter are not mere 'one hour gap-fillers'. They are designed to explore the Christian faith, to expose our human nature, and to contrast the values of the world with those of the gospel.

They sound dangerous!
Because the players will be widely spread, the organiser needs to take certain precautions. If there is any chance of local people or police being alarmed, consult them before you play the game. It is wise to place a reliable person as an observer/ umpire in each unit of players, in case of emer-gency. All players should know where to seek first aid or other assistance.

Why use them?
Like all the learning activities in this book, wide games pack a spiritual punch. Almost all of them have a strong 'simulation' flavour. In every case lots of excitement and exercise are involved; and because players use all their senses, they tend to remember the lesson of the game for a long time. The sheer pressure of an intense wide-game causes masks to drop, and players learn a lot about themselves and others. For this reason, wide games are best played by an existing community which can spend plenty of time thinking over the experience, e.g. a group which meets weekly, or which is away for a residential conference.

How to debrief a wide game
A wide game needs to be discussed after it has been run, or players may not even notice the main teaching points. This process of reflecting on the game is called 'debriefing'. When the game has aimed to 'simulate' a powerful life-experience (e.g., war, injustice), there will be a mass of emotions and insights to be shared. I like to spend about an hour doing a debriefing. However, a very simple game might only need 30 minutes, and a very intense one might need 1.5 hours. Beware of being too brief — or boring! Here is a useful framework.

1. Finish the game
Help players to realise that the game has ended. Remove all uniforms or team markings. After providing a brief time for toilet visits and drinks, call the group together in a large meeting area. Seat them in a circle, and tell them what you are about to do. Explain that comments are to be restricted to the topic being discussed and assure players that all aspects of the game will be covered. To control discussion, pass a microphone (it need not be a real one) around the group and insist that only the person with the mike can speak.

2. Share the experience
Allow members of each team, and officials, to share their feelings and experiences - before the game, at key points of the game, and at the end. Prevent players from analysing the game at this stage - what you want is simply a review of the game's highlights

and a feel for its emotional impact.

3. Reflect on the experience
Confine discussion to the game itself, but encourage players to look critically at things like teamwork, leadership styles, pressure, planning and servanthood as they were experienced during the game. Don't panic if some painful truths are exposed. Keep the criticism constructive, however, and follow up any special problems later. Counselling may be needed for the team leader who failed, or for the player who lost his temper. All this can be very helpful for personal growth.

4. Relate the game to the real world
Look at ways in which the game truly simulated life in 'the real world'. Ask players if they feel better able to understand or cope with some of the pressures of life today. For example, teenagers may discover that life at the top as a leader can be very lonely. Thus the lesson is to support community leaders, rather than continually undermine them.

5. Look at the faith lessons
You may prefer to merge this into the section the game. For example, if the game has featured widespread cheating, show that God is well aware of what human nature is like.

6. Wind it up, and down
Bring the group together, thank them for their co-operation, and announce point scores (if any) in a low-key manner. Summarise the main lessons from the game, then finish with a simple time of worship. This could involve prayer, readings, music and singing. Dismiss the group, provide time for relaxation and counsel any players who remain upset.

1. The cheating game

10 - 25   3 - 4 hours   12 - 200

DESCRIPTION

This energetic game can help a group explore a new campsite and build relationships. It starts as a simple orienteering race, but then widespread cheating sets in. At the end of the race, the cheating is slowly exposed. The penalty for cheating is severe, so everyone makes excuses. This leads into a look at the way Adam and Eve tried to 'cheat' God, and how feeble their excuses were. The message is that all people have fallen short of God's standards and need what Jesus offers.

CHECKLIST

- Maps of playing area for each team and for each official (see Samples)
- Copies of rules for each official.
- Score cards and pens — one for each team.
- Checkpoint markers (bearing a message)
- Prize.
- Costumes for trial scenes.
- Bibles for each participant.
- Copies of discussion questions for each discussion leader (see Samples)

PREPARATION

1 Produce a simple map of the playing area, using letters of the alphabet to mark the checkpoints that must be visited. Each team of players and each umpire or cheating agent will need a copy. It must be just possible for a very determined team to visit every point in the time allowed. A few of these checkpoints must be unpleasant or difficult to reach (e.g. one kilometre up a steep track). You could scatter the competitors by marking each team's map with a different 'first checkpoint' so that the teams start the race from different points.

2 Place distinctive markers at each of the checkpoints, each labelled with a different letter of the alphabet, as indicated on the map. These also bear a simple code-word (e.g. Foxtrot), or give interesting historical information about the site (e.g. old dairy). Simple score cards will be needed, so that competitors can record their codes/information.

3 Secretly brief some players and umpires to act as 'cheating agents' whose task is to offer false checkpoint information to other players. For example, they could pretend to have just been to the end of the steep one kilometre track.

4 Appoint handful of energetic umpires who will be available to offer first-aid, and to explain maps, rules etc, once the game is underway.

5 Brief appropriate people to be time-keepers, scrutineers (of the result slips), barristers and court officials for the final trials.

6 Display a splendid prize before the activity begins. One group made up a certificate which offered the winner freedom from doing any chores for the duration of the weekend camp.

7 Appropriate people should be ready to run a Bible study on topics such as sin, judgment and forgiveness. See Samples.

RUNNING THE ACTIVITY

This is how the game might run:

12.00 Give a brief pep-talk about the competitive 'information race/orienteering competition' which is to follow lunch. Display the prize, or certificate, to be won.

1.00 Final inspection (or erection) of all checkpoint markers. Final (top secret) briefing of 'cheating agents' and officials.

2.00 Assemble all participants and divide them into teams. These teams could be pairs, or even individuals, if safety is not a problem,

WIDE GAMES

but cheating is more likely if teams of 4-6 people are used. Explain the rules (see below), issue a score card and map to each team, and start the race. The umpires can keep the excitement high by reminding competitors of the limited time available. As time runs out, teams tend to gather checkpoint information by asking officials and other competitors instead of visiting checkpoints. This is illegal.

2.45 Timekeepers announce the finish of the game. Provide cool drinks; then collect score cards. Note the finishing time, the accuracy, and the amount of cheating evident on each card. Cheating is evident as wrong codes or information on the score cards.

3.00 With great ceremony, announce the winning team and their finishing time. At the very moment of awarding the prize, one of the officials should call out and accuse the winners of cheating. Announce that the prize will go to the team with the next best finishing time; an official again interrupts with the accusation of cheating. Repeat this process until all teams admit to having cheated by accepting information from others.

3.30 Announce that a trial is to take place and explain that barristers are available to help teams evade conviction and punishment. Drop hints that the judge will be fair but severe, depriving the guilty of valued privileges. After allowing each team to brief their own barrister, run a realistic mock-trial, with a suitably stern and fair judge. Once all have been declared guilty, and just before a sentence can be passed down, interrupt the trial and do the Bible study.

4.15 Hand out Bibles, form small discussion groups and look at the discussion questions.

4.45 Reflect on the whole game together. It is just as important to deal with any hurt feelings as it is to explore the theology. Those involved as 'cheating agents' may need to express how painful it was to act in that role, etc. See 'How to debrief' on page 12.

5.00 Close off with some quiet prayer and/or singing. Provide some free time and watch for people who are still upset by the game.

ESSENTIAL RULES

1 Players must stay in their teams.

2 Players must gather information from the official checkpoint markers only. (Display a sample marker.)

3 Each team must first go to the checkpoint which is specially marked on their team map. After finding this point, the team is free to choose its own route.

4 When time is up, all teams must return promptly to the starting point so that cards can be checked. No furthr information can be recorded once playing time has ended.

5 The prize will be awarded to the team which has finished inside the time limit and in the best time, and which has all the checkpoint marker information accurately recorded.

SAMPLES

Map

Your sketch map could be as simple as the one on page 16.

Questions

These would suit teenagers or adults.

- Genesis 3:1,3. Why is the command of Genesis 2:16-17 misquoted?
- Genesis 3:5-6. Why did Eve sin? Why involve Adam?
- Genesis 3:12-13. Who do Adam and Eve blame for their actions?
- In what ways do we resemble Adam and Eve in our behaviour? Think back to the game we have just played.
- Romans 3:23. Do all humans fall below God's standards? Why?
- Romans 3:24. Why did Jesus have to come to die?

VARIATIONS

1 The playing area can be as small or as large as required, but must allow teams to keep meeting each other, otherwise information will not be illegally exchanged.

2 For checkpoints you could use concealed orienteering markers, requiring the use of map and compass.

3 If the game is played on the first day of a conference or camp at an unfamiliar site, you can use it to familiarise everyone with the boundaries, regulations and facilities of the property by ensuring that the checkpoints take players to the important parts of the site.

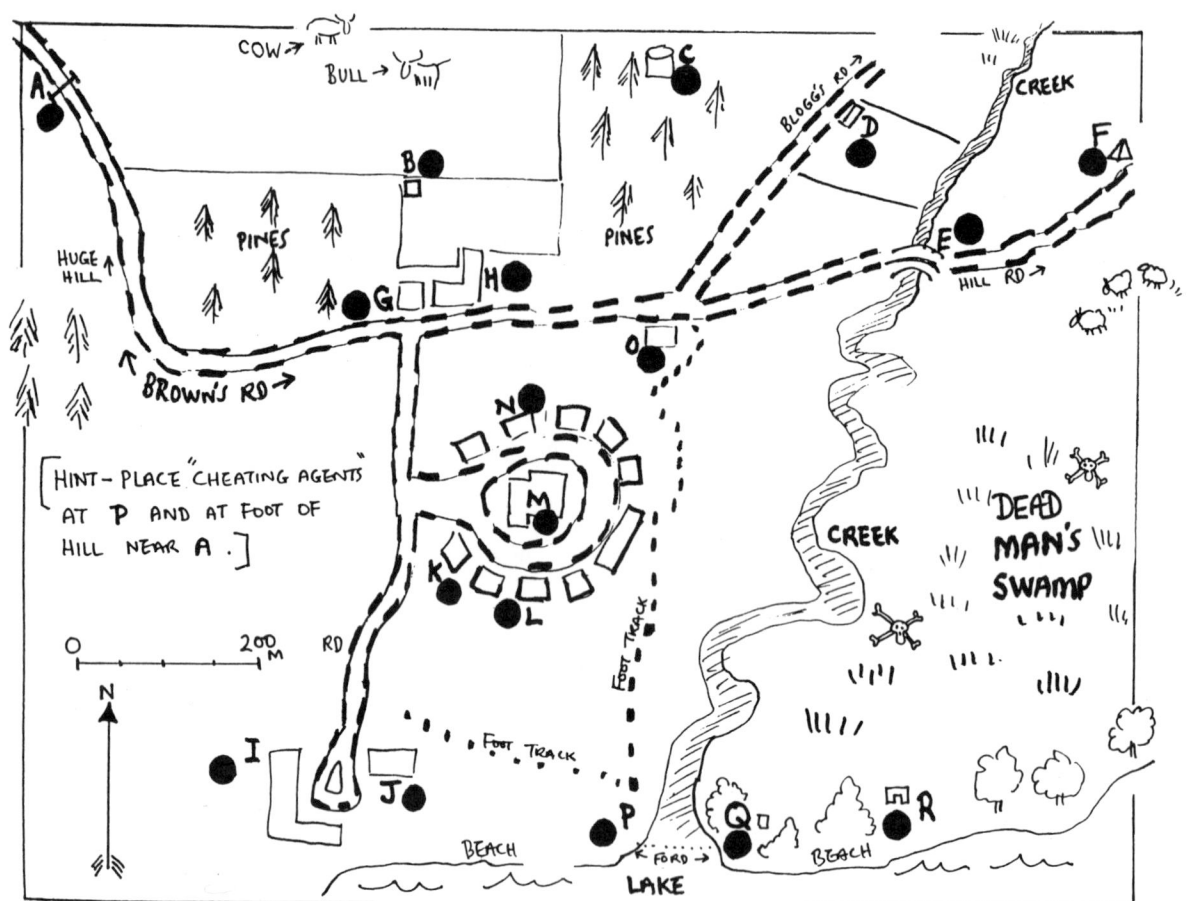

2. The Prophet of Truth

16 -100   3 - 4 hours   16 - 200

DESCRIPTION

This emotionally powerful game helps players understand the urgency of the need for evangelism, the attraction of false faiths, and the communication problems faced by the Church. Competing teams roam local streets in search of the 'Prophet of Truth'; on the way they meet 'false prophets' who present attractive values and life-styles. The team who finally locate the Prophet of Truth are the winners; their reward is a feast. Before they can relax, however, they are urged to go and tell all the others. The closing scenes are dramatic, because some teams refuse to believe the warnings, return too late — and find themselves locked out of the banquet! It's exciting, exhausting and unforgettable.

CHECKLIST

- Copies of a map of the area — for each team and each official.
- Copies of rules — issue as above.
- Written clues for teams, in sealed envelopes.
- Instructions for officials (umpires, prophets, banquet group).
- Props and costumes as required by the various prophets.
- Lipstick marker for the Prophet of Truth.
- Decorated hall, complete with party food.
- Bibles for all participants.

PREPARATION

1 The ideal playing area is a square kilometre of suburbia, but a rural location is adequate. Produce maps of the area with enough detail to challenge the ability of the players. Choose locations on the map for the various prophets.

2 Invent 'clues' which will direct teams to each site. Write out clues, photocopy so that each team will have a complete set, and seal each clue in a separate envelope. Label each team's set of clues with the team name, and number them consecutively. Keep first clues for issue at the start of the game; issue the remainder to the false prophets. If you organise these clues and envelopes so that each team follows a different 'circuit' of the false prophets, this stops the game from degenerating into 'follow the leader'. The last envelope for each team should direct them to the real Prophet.

3 Visit the area, if possible, and inspect the locations. Ensure that teams are able to cover the territory in the allotted time, remembering that they will need time to talk with the 'prophets', and to discuss the clues. Assume that teams will move at a steady walking pace.

4 Appoint the key officials and discuss their various roles with them. You will need to provide written instructions and resources for the following.

- Umpires, who each accompany a team and enforce the rules. If a group is slow to locate their first false prophet, the umpire may direct them there.

- False prophets, who represent 'attractive' non-Christian lifestyles (e.g. materialist, pleasure-seeker, Marxist, environmental extremist, New-Age follower). Each of these must try hard to 'sell' their beliefs, and to convince teams that they are the Prophet of Truth. As soon as a team rejects their claims, false prophets should hand over the next clue in that team's set. False prophets will need time to develop their speeches and to prepare any props. They may

also need an appropriate companion if the area presents safety problems.
- The Prophet of Truth, who needs a speech and props to be convincing; a marker (lipstick) to put a cross on the winning team's foreheads; and a copy of some special instructions to give them. To avoid discovery the Prophet of Truth must be positioned well clear of the false prophets. The Prophet needs some means to get back to the Heavenly Banquet Hall in order to greet the winning team on their arrival.

5 Brief some people to set up the Heavenly Banquet. They could set it up in the same room that players depart from (after they leave). The Banquet team must work fast, setting up extravagant decorations and food. The ideal room has a heavy door opening onto an outside drive or lawn, and numerous windows doing likewise. The idea is that when 'Heaven's Door' closes, the feast is very visible to those locked outside, who are unable to force their way inside past the door and the staff.

6 Select teams each with 6-8 members. At the start of the race each team will need its own map, copy of the rules and a first clue.

7 One or two people need to be fully prepared to run the debriefing session at the close of the game. See 'How to debrief' on page 12. This game generates powerful emotions and must be carefully concluded.

RUNNING THE ACTIVITY

This is how the game might run.
- 5.00 Explain the game before the evening meal and announce teams. This should help generate excitement. Hold a secret briefing of all officials, and ensure that all prophets know their locations.
- 7.00 Assemble all players. Give a final description of the game plus safety instructions. Issue maps, rules and sealed clues to all teams, allow time for toilet visits and place an umpire with each team. Deal with any final questions, and make sure players understand the need for secrecy regarding their clues. By now, all prophets must be in position.
- 7.30 Stage an exciting start, e.g. by making team leaders sprint to collect their first 'clue'. Teams will puzzle over their clues, then dash off to different destinations. The Heavenly Banquet could now be set up.
- 8.00 The game organiser could leave the banquet team to finish their task, and patrol the playing area to ensure that all is well.
- 8.15 The leading team should now be closing in on the Prophet of Truth, having located all the false prophets. The Prophet should greet them, convince them, mark some of them with a cross on the forehead, give them the marker, and before departing, hand over the following instructions: 'Heaven is the main hall back at base. Heaven's door closes at 8.45pm exactly. Admission is by the special mark on the forehead.' Normally the team will hastily mark each other then rush back to base, which should be 10-15 minutes away.
- 8.30 The Prophet must be at Heaven's Door to welcome the winning team and to ask accusingly 'Where are all the others?' The winners typically race out into the night to warn the other players and false prophets.
- 9.00 The Heavenly Gates swing shut, leaving the saintly to feast inside, and the doomed to peer sadly through the windows. It is vital to have adults outside who can control any hysteria, and who can encourage pitiful cries for help.
- 9.15 Announce that the game is over, call all players inside for supper, and ensure that they are fed well. Allow 15 minutes, then proceed to debriefing. (See 'How to debrief' on p. 12, and sample questions below.)
- 10.15 Wind down the evening with some quiet prayer and singing. Watch for people who are still upset. Allow time for showers and relaxed conversation before declaring bed-time.

ESSENTIAL RULES

1 Players must stay in their teams.
2 The umpires' word is law.
3 Each team is to follow its clue until it finds the prophet indicated. When you receive the next clue, repeat the process. The Prophet of Truth will give instructions which must be obeyed.
4 After 90 minutes the game ends. Players then return to base.
5 If first-aid is required, consult your umpire and arrange help.

SAMPLES

Questions

These could be part of the debriefing for older teens or adults.
- What were the leadership dynamics in your team? What caused some to lead and others to follow? What is Christian leadership?
- Did your group try to co-operate with other teams? Why not? What difference would it have made if all teams had shared information? What parallels can you see with the problem of divisions between churches?

- In what ways did the false prophets resemble voices you hear in the media? What can we do to avoid being brainwashed into non-Christian lifestyles? Identify the false prophets and say why they were not convincing.
- Why was the Prophet of Truth convincing? Why do so many people find Jesus to be convincing when they discover him?
- How do we convince people who have never met Jesus? What things stop us communicating effectively? How important is lifestyle in all this?
- Does Jesus mention Heaven and Hell in the Gospels, or do they belong to fairyland? What feelings did you have when some players were 'in' and some were locked 'outside'? What should be our motives for evangelism?
- Read and comment on these Bible passages. Warnings that evangelism may be rejected — Matthew 10:11-24. Warnings of false prophets — Matthew 24. Images of Heaven and Hell — Revelation 20:11-15, Luke 16: 19-31.

Clues

1 The clues to the locations of the prophets could be in rhyme to add a touch of class. The clue below pointed to the junction of McDonald St and Batterham Reserve.

'Where Scottish hamburger joins ham done in batter, this prophet's Reserved, but with you he'll chatter.'

The map provided was photocopied from a street directory.

2 In one game the Prophet of Truth had hymns playing in the background, and was majestic in flowing white robes. The first team to find her were instantly convinced, especially when she read the following to them from a gold scroll:

'Truth is my nature, and truth is my name,
I'll take you to Heaven, without sin or blame,
Heaven's at base, in the main meeting room,
Those left outside it must dwell in the gloom,
Hurry you must, for time's running out,
Heaven's doors close soon, you might be locked out,
To get in, your forehead must bear Heaven's mark,
Without it, rejected, you'll weep in the dark,
Away with you now, there is much you should do,
I'll meet you in Heaven, and share it with you.'

VARIATIONS

1 To add to the excitement of the start, you could arrange for the first clues to be read aloud to the teams — simultaneously — at dictation speed.

2 Make teams accurately name a false prophet before they receive the next clue. If the team doesn't know the 'ism' (e.g. hedonism), they could describe the lifestyle and offer reasons for rejecting it.

3 Umpires or prophets could give each team the clue for the Prophet of Truth at an agreed time. This gives a close finish to the race.

CROSS REFERENCE

An indoor simulation game in the next chapter, 'Sell it if you can' raises many similar issues, and could be played a few days after this game.

3. The great haggis hunt

10 - 100   6 - 24 hours   16 - 200

DESCRIPTION

This game teaches that the Church needs to make full use of all the gifts given to its members. Teamwork and co-operation are shown to be essential and the damaging effects of needless competition can also be highlighted. The game leads into a Bible study on the need for unity and for recognition of each other's gifts.

Competing teams set up concealed campsites in a lightly forested area. (For a half-day activity, an urban setting may be used.) The members of each team are given distinct roles — some navigate while others take charge of shelter construction or strategy. The teams attempt to locate each other's sites, and to gain an authentic sighting of the elusive feral haggis which haunts the area. Junior groups especially, seem to enjoy the extra adrenalin of watching for 'something' in the dark. Night-time sentries add to the drama.

CHECKLIST

- Copies of a map of the area — for each team and for each official (see Samples)
- Copies of rules — distribute as above.
- Orders for teams, in sealed envelopes.
- Food, shelter and transport (as required for playing area).
- Identification materials for players and team bases.
- First aid equipment.
- Bibles for all participants.

PREPARATION

1 Locate a suitable playing area with safe, well-defined boundaries.

2 Visit the area, choose locations for the bases/campsites, and produce an appropriately detailed map.

3 Appoint umpires for each team, roving umpires, and first-aiders. Issue the team umpires with a copy of the point scoring system (see Samples). A small group may also be needed to transport food and equipment. These people need to be fully briefed on the nature and purpose of the game and they should have written rules, instructions and maps.

4 Select teams, each with 6—18 members. Each team will need its own map, copy of the rules and sealed orders. If groups of youngsters require supervision, you could give extra adults the role of playing team-members who do not 'lead' unless safety is at risk.

5 One or more people need to be fully prepared to run the debriefing session at the end of the game. See 'How to debrief' on page 12.

6 If appropriate, some adults might be encouraged to arrange for 'sightings' of the fearsome feral haggis. I am told that a mixture of muffled bagpipes and tiger growls should suffice. One group arranged for a piper in full highland dress to stroll through the playing area at 1.00 am, with dramatic results.

7 The food and equipment required will vary according to local conditions. If the site is bounded by roads, it is easy to deliver shelter materials (e.g. tarpaulins, ropes) and food supplies by car. If cooking in the playing area is not an option, provide picnic-style rations.

RUNNING THE ACTIVITY

This is how the game might run over a 20-24 hour period. The times below relate to a game played with 11-year-olds in late summer.

10.00 (am) Describe the game to all players,

WIDE GAMES

allowing time for questions and discussion. Hold final briefings for umpires, first-aiders, and other key workers. Announce teams. All this may only need an hour.

11.00 Allow teams to meet and to organise personal gear. This may need an hour. Players could then be involved in other activities while game organisers attend to the last minute details.

2.00 (pm) Meeting of all players and officials after lunch. Synchronise watches. Issue rules, maps, sealed orders and supplies to each team. Allocate and explain the specialised roles: navigators (lead teams to campsites), builders (construct an adequate shelter), camouflagers (render shelters invisible to rival teams), cooks (organise rations) and strategists (plan tactics for discovering other teams and sites). Answer any questions. It may be wise to identify teams by using spectacular 'face-paint' decorations. This could be done now, or on arrival at the secret bases.

3.00 Teams set off to their campsites, following specified routes. This ensures that no group 'accidentally' comes across the campsite of another team. The 'Navigators' should lead each group at this stage.

4.00 Teams arrive at the designated campsites, and the members perform their allotted tasks. The specialist groups must be allowed to maintain control over their areas of responsibility, even though they may ask the others to help.

5.30 Teams could now open sealed orders, and enjoy a meal. The Strategists announce their plan and call on the Navigators to help.

6.00 Half of the teams (as per the sealed orders) guard their bases while the other teams are allowed to leave their sites and go out searching for them. Points are awarded by the umpires for locating other sites or teams. Defending teams score points by evading detection and by spotting other teams.

7.30 Roles are reversed, with hunters becoming the hunted.

9.00 Nightfall, supper and bed. Points could be awarded for any teams which maintain a sentry for part (or all) of the night. The role of night sentry is usually most memorable, especially if the area features nocturnal animal life. Points are scored if the dreaded feral haggis is seen or heard, and the umpire is roused in time to confirm the event.

1.00 (am) If necessary, send out a pair of creative adults to ensure that each team has a convincing encounter with the feral haggis.

6.00 All groups rise, pack, return to starting point.

7.00 Remove all team identification. Communal breakfast, followed by the debriefing. Follow the debriefing with showers and a relaxed pack-up operation. The rest of the day's program should allow for people's tiredness.

ESSENTIAL RULES

1 Players must stay with their teams at all times.
2 The umpires' word is law.
3 Teams must follow all written or verbal instructions given to them by the organisers.
4 No player is to move outside the boundaries of the playing area.
5 Teams must observe all time-limits and deadlines.
6 If first-aid is required, players must consult their umpire and arrange help.

SAMPLES

Sealed orders

Your team is to guard your base from 6.00-7.30 pm, and to go searching from 7.30-9.00 pm. You must then remain at your base until 6.00 am.'

Scoring system

The scoring system could be as follows:
- Setting up an approved shelter (average height 1 metre) = 50 points
- Camouflaging shelter adequately (invisible at 20m) = 50 points
- Finding another team's site = 100 points per site.
- Spotting another team = 50 points (awarded once per team)
- Reporting the approach of a feral haggis to team's umpire = 100 points
- Maintaining a night sentry = 10 points per hour.
- Returning to team's base before the deadline = 25 points

Debriefing questions

Some main points to explore are as follows:
- Which of the specialist groups was the most important?
- Could any of the specialist groups have been completely dropped?
- Was each specialist group, in fact, a vital part of the team?
- Why did the different teams compete against each other?
- Would they have scored more points by co-operating with the other teams? (Note that the rules must only hint at the need to compete. Usually all players will treat the whole exercise as fiercely competitive.)
- Explore some biblical passages which teach the need to respect the gifts of others and to maintain unity in the Church. Suitable material to

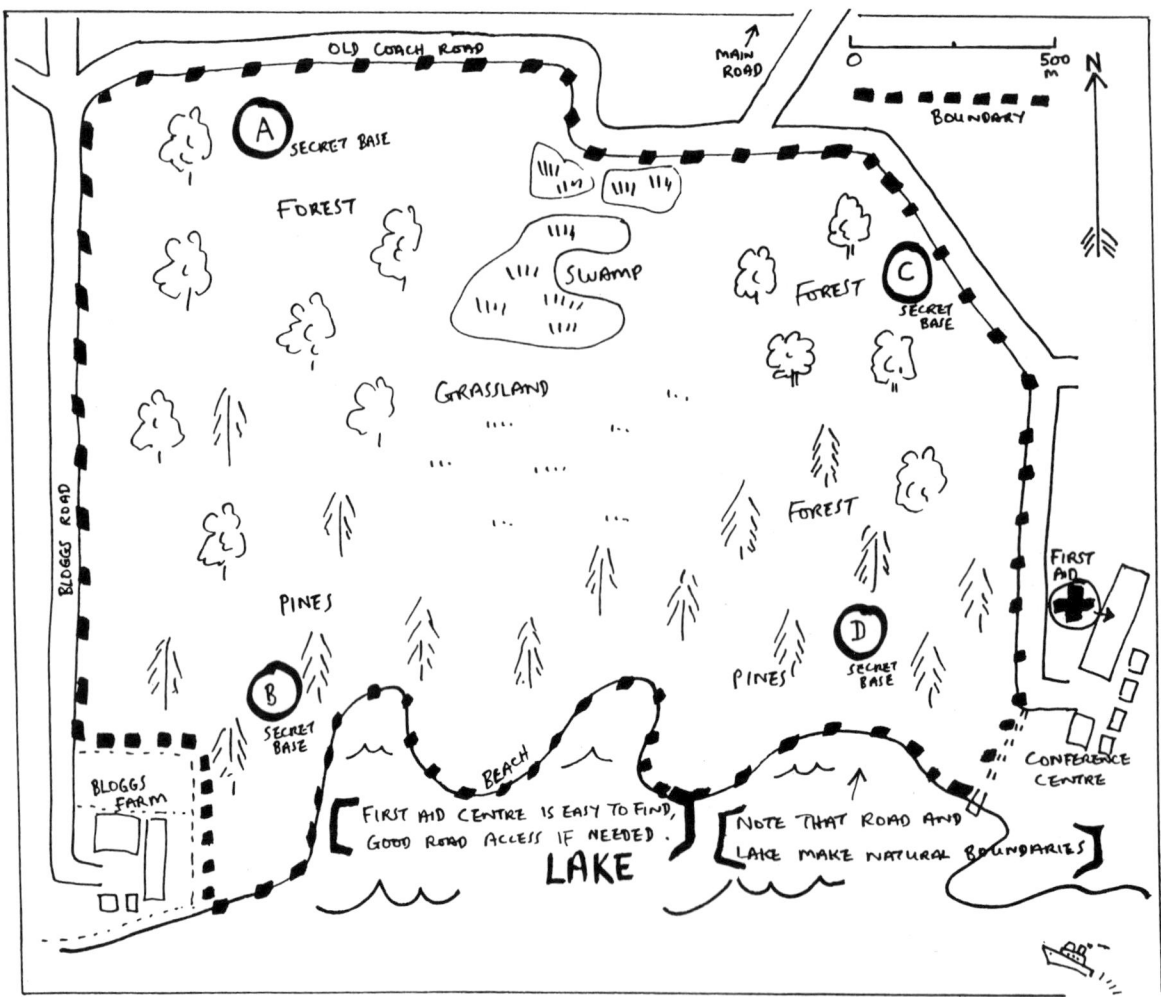

explore might include John 17:20-23 (Christ's prayer for the unity of his Church), 1 Corinthians 12 (Paul's call to a strife-torn church, using the image of the 'body' to stress the value of each gift and each church member), and Romans 12:3-8 (more on the value of each gift). Obviously, these passages would require very different handling for different groups. A simple drama or mime would make this material digestible for even young teens. Matur Christians might want to explore it in considerable depth.

Playing area

A suitable playing area might look like the one shown above.

VARIATIONS

1 Roving umpires could inspect the various campsites at 5.30pm to ensure that all shelters are up to a specified standard. Points could be awarded for design and camouflage.

2 First aiders could roam about, patrol by car, or stay at an agreed location. All participants need ready access to help.

3 If the game is to be a half-day version, shelters could be replaced with a flag or cluster of balloons. Something is needed to mark each site.

4 You could replace the 'feral haggis' with some other beast, or simply omit it.

5 You could add an orienteering flavour by providing compasses and detailed maps.

4. Life is not a picnic

10 - 100   2 - 3 hours   16 - 200

DESCRIPTION

In this game players discover what sacrificial giving is, and can then explore biblical teaching on justice, poverty and possessions. Many of them will fall into the trap of being selfish and greedy. Players head off in small groups to different locations, looking forward to enjoying a picnic lunch and unaware that they are taking part in a simulation experience. On opening their food boxes, some groups discover abundance, while others face a lean time. As the game proceeds, the 'rich' groups discover the problems of the 'poor', and must decide whether to ignore them or to help.

CHECKLIST

- A simple map for each group, showing where they are to have lunch,
- Picnic lunch supplies for 'rich' and 'poor' groups, sealed in boxes (see Sample menus)
- A note from the cooks, for each group's food box (see Samples)
- Bibles for all participants.

PREPARATION

1 Choose locations for each group to eat their picnic meal. Groups should be out of sight of each other, but within 2 minutes walk of some other groups.

2 Plan the groups so that one capable adult is present in each. These people should be the only ones in their groups to know that the picnic is to be a simulation experience; they are 'undercover' umpires and need to be well briefed.

3 The groups are to be equal in size (maximum of twelve per group), and could be made up from existing small groups. Half of these groups will be the 'rich', and half the 'poor'. Each 'rich' group is to have a 'poor' group placed nearby.

4 The food for each group could be delivered to the picnic sites, or issued as groups head off. In the latter case, ensure that the boxes are similar in weight and volume, and that they are thoroughly taped shut. Mark each box clearly with the group's name. No clue must be given that this is a simulation/wide game.

5 A box for 'the rich' should contain more food than the group could eat, including plenty of luxury items (e.g. sweets, chocolates, soft drinks, desserts). There should be so much that the group could share with a 'poor' group and still be adequately nourished. Include some canned food, but no can opener. This will be explained below.

6 Obviously, the boxes for 'the poor' will contain meagre supplies — plain drinking water, some very plain sandwiches, and some boring biscuits would be ideal. Don't make it so inadequate that people realise a game is involved; there should be enough to provide a very light meal for all. Put a can opener in each box, but no cans.

7 Each group needs a map which guides them to their picnic spot and indicates the positions of other groups. In each food box, place 'a note from the cooks'. The 'rich' groups have a note telling them to go to a specified neighbouring group to borrow a can-opener. These neighbours will, in every case, be 'poor' groups; the 'poor' have a note telling them to expect such a visit.

8 A number of people need to be fully prepared to run the debriefing session at the end of the game. (See 'How to debrief' on page 12.) This game can generate some very intense emotions, so conclude it carefully.

RUNNING THE ACTIVITY

This is how the game might run.

12.00 (Noon) Prepare and seal up the picnic boxes. Ensure that none of the participants see this process.

1.00 Assemble the participants and explain that they are to have a surprise picnic lunch. If necessary, allow time for toilet visits and clothing changes. Then announce the groups and send them off, asking them to stay in their exclusive picnic locations until 2.00 pm and then return to the meeting place.

1.10 Groups will arrive at their locations, aided by their maps. They open the food box provided, and read the note from the cooks. There will be some strong reactions from the 'poor', but the umpires present should play things down, and comment 'Mmmm, the cooks must have been on a tight budget for this meal!' Within minutes, the 'rich' will be sending messengers to their designated neighbours. The shrewd ones will size up the situation, borrow the can opener, and return with the news that 'The suckers over there have got nothing.' Typically a brief debate will follow, and the 'rich' will decide to share nothing, something, or the lot.

1.30 By now many of the 'poor' will be aware of the different standards of food. They may try to beg for help, or to 'rent' out their can opener. It will be more effective if the groups themselves remain stationary, but send messengers. This is a very important stage in the game. The politics can become quite tense.

2.00 All groups are to return to the main meeting area, and the debriefing begins. Explore the events and emotions of the game thoroughly; and cover the desired biblical material (see Sample questions and Bible references).

3.00 Wind up the discussion with some quiet prayer and singing. The 'rich' should then serve the 'poor' with a generous afternoon tea before joining them. This defuses any hard feelings and ensures that no-one is left hungry. Allow time for some relaxed games and conversation before launching into your next major activity. Watch for any players who are still upset.

ESSENTIAL RULES

These are so simple that they could be given verbally.

1 Picnic groups should go to their designated sites, open boxes, and stay there until it is time to return.

2 If a problem arises, each group may send one messenger to visit other groups.

SAMPLES

Menu

- For the 'rich': 2 large bread rolls each, loads of fillings, fresh fruit, chocolate bars, sweets, cakes, fancy biscuits, soft drinks, cans of fruit juice, canned fruit. Supply crockery and cutlery, but no can opener.
- For the 'poor': 2 slices of bread per person, spread with jam or similar; plain drinking water, some boring biscuits, and a can opener. Supply cups, but no plates or cutlery.

Notes from the cooks

- Rich groups could be told: 'Dear group, we appear to be out of can-openers. Please go to group number ... and ask to borrow theirs.'
- Poor groups could be told: 'Dear group, if a neighbouring group wants to borrow some of your picnic equipment, please ensure that it comes back to the kitchen in this box.'

Questions

Here are some possible questions and Bible references.

- When did your group realise that the food supplies were 'rigged'?
- Did you work out the reason for this during the game?
- How did your group respond to the situation?
- What relationship developed between you and your neighbouring group?
- What did it feel like to share/not share?
- In what ways is the game a parable of life in the wider world?
- How would Jesus want us to organise the world's resources?
- What can we learn from the following Bible passages?
  Leviticus 25 (Explain the cultural background as necessary).
  Jeremiah 34, 52 (Note the failure and the punishment).
  Matthew 25:31-46.
  James 2:14-19, 5:1-5.
  Acts 11:28-30.

If you need more resources on this topic, contact a Christian overseas aid agency (e.g. TEAR Australia, PO Box 289, Hawthorn Vic 3122 or World Vision, 161 Sturt St, Melbourne Vic 3000) and ask for educational material.

VARIATIONS

1 You could make the game more severe by giving the 'poor' totally inadequate supplies, and ensuring that they are powerless to demand justice. Lengthening the playing time also adds drama. The version above is designed to be subtle, so that the reality of the situation slowly dawns on the players.

2 If educated adults are playing, you could give the contents of the boxes hidden meaning. For

WIDE GAME

example, the 'rich' could have food and technology, but be short of energy (no gas for the stove). Some of the 'poor' groups could be rich in energy (spare gas cylinders) or in raw materials (uncooked food?). You could cover the economics of world poverty during the debriefing (or later in the day).

CROSS REFERENCE

See 'Help for Slobovia' (overleaf) for a more complex game on this topic.

5. Help for Slobovia

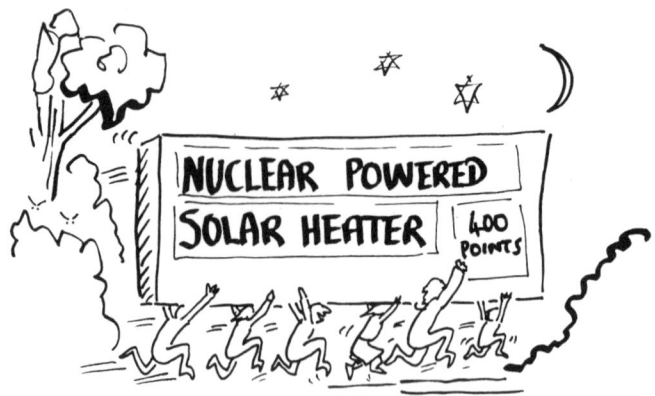

14 - 30   4 - 24 hours   20 - 200

DESCRIPTION

This complex game confronts players with the issues of world poverty and foreign aid. Players find themselves belonging to a wealthy nation (Upper Slobovia), a poor nation (Lower Slobovia), or an aggressive terrorist group (the Slobovian unPopular Liberation Front — SPLF). The teams set up bases and get involved in smuggling, foreign aid, warfare and peacemaking. This game is best played over a large area, and may feature complex tactics, close teamwork, and advanced bushcraft skills. There is a trap: the wealthy nation will be tempted to smuggle high technology to the poor nation, rather than give what is really needed.

CHECKLIST

- Copies of a map of the area — for each team and each umpire and UN official (see Samples).
- Copies of rules — distributed as above.
- Duplicate copies of telegrams for UN officials (see Samples).
- Sealed orders for each team, and copies for each umpire (see Samples)
- Food (in sealed boxes) and shelter for all participants.
- Labelled cartons (see Samples), packing tape, signs, face paint for team identification and armbands.
- Bibles for all participants.
- Lanterns (for overnight game).
- First Aid supplies.

PREPARATION

1 Produce maps of a suitable playing area, measuring about 0.5 by 1 kilometre (see Samples). Although undulating forest is ideal, farmland or even urban settings can be used. Get permission from owners or local authorities, as appropriate. Well-defined boundaries are a must. Make sure that the specified locations for the various bases are suitably concealed.

2 Appoint the following people and brief them on the game's nature and purpose: umpires for each of the three teams, roving umpires, and United Nations officials. They should also be in charge of first aid. They will need written rules, sealed orders, telegrams and maps (see Samples). Team umpires need a copy of the point scoring system (see Samples), and must record in writing all points earned by their team.

3 Select teams of even ability and with 6-18 members each. To manage large numbers place a number of self-contained units of 18 on each team. Every team will need a map, a copy of the rules and sealed orders. If groups of youngsters require supervision, give extra adults the role of 'playing-umpires' who do not lead unless safety is at risk.

4 One or more people need to be fully prepared to run the debriefing session at the end of the game. See 'how to debrief' on page 12.

5 The food and equipment required will vary according to local conditions. Players may need to carry their supplies, or deliveries could be made by car. Shelters could be tents or tarpaulins. Overnight games may require lantern, torches, and robust protective clothing.

6 If cooking is not appropriate, supply picnic-style rations. Seal food supplies in boxes labelled with team names. Because the three teams have distinctive roles, their food varies. Upper Slobovia will have nearly

WIDE GAMES

enough food (including luxury items) to meet both its own needs and those of impoverished Lower Slobovia; poor Lower Slobovia will have about half of what it needs and the SPLF terrorists will have adequate food. So that players do not discover that the food rations have been set up this way, ensure that food boxes stay tightly sealed until play has started.

7 Upper Slobovia will also need a large supply of cardboard cartons, which may be smuggled during the game. If supplied flat, these cartons must be reconstructed and strongly taped before being moved. They should be appropriately labelled (see Samples).

RUNNING THE ACTIVITY

This is how the game might run over a 20-24 hour period. Note that it can be equally effective as a half-day activity. The times given below relate to a game played in autumn with 15-16 year olds.

9.00 (am) Describe the game to all players, allowing time for questions and discussion. Announce teams, but not roles. Final briefings for umpires, officials, helpers and first-aiders. All this may only need an hour.

10.00 Run other activities during the morning, but allow participants to think about the game and to prepare personal gear. The officials may need this time to make final preparations.

2.00 (pm) Give the three teams maps and rules. They head off to designated secret bases. Food and equipment is delivered/carried.

3.00 Teams arrive at their respective bases, and umpires hand over the sealed envelopes which reveal their roles for the first time. Teams plan tactics, erect camouflaged shelters to the required standard set out in the rules and paint each other's faces.

4.00 Play begins. Teams will want to locate the bases of their rivals and familiarise themselves with the boundaries. Smuggling of foreign aid boxes gets underway, and guards are posted. The SPLF are permitted to raid Lower Slobovia between 5.00-5.20 pm. Prisoners report to the UN, and are later returned to the game. Umpires busily keep scores (see Samples).

6.00 Teams must be back at sites. Mealtime and rest period. By now the populations of both Slobovias will be aware of the food inequality, due to telegrams which are delivered by UN officials (see Samples), and box inspection.

7.30 Play resumes. SPLF permitted to raid LS between 8.00-8.20pm. Members of LS will be begging for food, not empty boxes!

10.30 Teams must be back at sites. Compulsory sleeping time 11.00-5.00am.

6.00 Play resumes.

7.30 Teams must be back at sites. Breakfast is eaten and the site packed up.

8.30 Teams leave sites, and return to a suitable debriefing area.

9.30 Players remove face-paint, have a snack, then join in the debriefing. See 'How to debrief' on page 12 and questions in Samples. Afterwards distribute educational kits from groups such as TEAR Australia or World Vision to all players. Discuss possible projects the group could take on. Close with music and prayer. Allow time for showers, unpacking, and rest.

ESSENTIAL RULES

- At all times, every player must be attached to a group which includes an umpire.
- Any player absent from a group for over 5 minutes will be declared 'dead'. The player must be found, and accompanied by the whole group to the UN for imprisonment (which lasts 20 minutes). The group may return later to collect them. There will be a points penalty for each such collection.
- The above rule applies to any player who is legally 'tagged' by a rival.
- The umpires' word is law. Legal points may be clarified at the UN.
- The personal property of rival team members is not to be interfered with.
- Any breach of time limits loses points. Teams must be at their bases except during playing times of 4.00-6.00 pm, 7.30-10.30 pm, and 6.00-7.30 am.
- First aid problems must be reported to the nearest umpire. Only the official foreign aid boxes may be smuggled, and these must never be collapsed, folded or squashed.
- Any pilfered tarps/tents must be handed in to the UN within half an hour, and may be redeemed at great cost by the owners.
- Groups must use the supplied tarpaulins/tents to construct shelters which provide adequate cover and average 1 metre in height. These shelters are to remain erect (as above) for the duration of the game.

SAMPLES

Sealed orders for Upper Slobovians

- You are safe from SPLF capture only when in your own territory. The SPLF may capture you and confiscate any boxes carried, but must then release you.
- You may earn points only by smuggling foreign aid boxes to L S.
- You may not pilfer or interfere with SPLF boxes or tarps.

Sealed orders for Lower Slobovians

- You may be captured by the SPLF if you enter their territory. This means that you lose any boxes/tarps you are carrying. It also means that you are 'dead', and must be taken by your group to the UN. (Your umpire will grant you safe passage to the UN to deliver the 'dead'. You may call back later to collect such persons, but at your own risk.)
- You are safe inside your own territory, except when the SPLF make their two short raids (see rules for SPLF). On these raids they may capture you for the sole purpose of confiscating boxes or tarps. You do not 'lose a life'.
- You are totally safe when inside Upper Slobovia.
- You earn points by safely stockpiling boxes (delivered to your territory by the US), and by pilfering tarps and boxes (from the SPLF).

Sealed orders for the SPLF

- You earn points by capturing trespassers on your land. Those from US lose any boxes or tarps they are carrying, and go free. Those from LS lose such items and also lose a life.
- You also earn points by confiscating boxes or tarps found during your two raids into LS territory (between 5.00-5.20 pm, and 8.00-8.20 pm).
- You must be alert lest the Lower Slobovians pilfer your boxes or tarps.

Boxes

The boxes supplied to Upper Slobovia could range in size from shoe boxes to refrigerator cartons. The smuggling value of each should be clearly marked and linked to how absurdly 'high-tech' the contents are. Sample labels on boxes are:
- Nuclear-powered porta-potty, 500 points.
- Megadeath Supremo tank-launcher, 450 points.
- Coal-fired solar-heating system, 400 points.
- Twin-turbo, Mach III, presidential limousine, 350 points.
- Wind-operated Coca-Cola factory, 250 points.
- Scented toothpaste factory, 100 points.
- Self-help food-growing kit, 25 points.

Telegrams

Just as the first meal is due to start, the UN officials could deliver these telegrams:
- (To the Upper Slobovians) — 'Famine has struck in Lower Slobovia. If you wish to help, you may send supplies now, under safe escort by the UN. You may prefer to respond at a later date, or not at all.'
- (To the Lower Slobovians) — 'Reports have reached the UN that famine has struck in your land. The following UN telegram has just been delivered to Upper Slobovia (quote the above). The UN is hoping for a generous response to its appeal. The UN has no emergency supplies at its headquarters.'

Playing area

A playing area like the one shown below would be ideal.

Discussion questions

Some interesting points to explore are:
- What did each team see as their main task?
- How did they view the other teams?
- How powerful/powerless did teams feel?
- How well was the food problem handled?
- Were boxes more important than food?
- In real life, how does war affect the poorer countries?
- In real life, is foreign aid always well managed from all sides?
- How do groups like TEAR Australia or World Vision ensure that their aid is well used?
- Should charity begin and end at home?
- What does the Bible say about concern for the poor? (Explore Matthew 25:31-46, Acts 6:1-2, 1 Corinthians 16:1-4, Amos 4:1 and 5:11-12, Micah 6:8-16, 1 John 3:16-18 and so on)

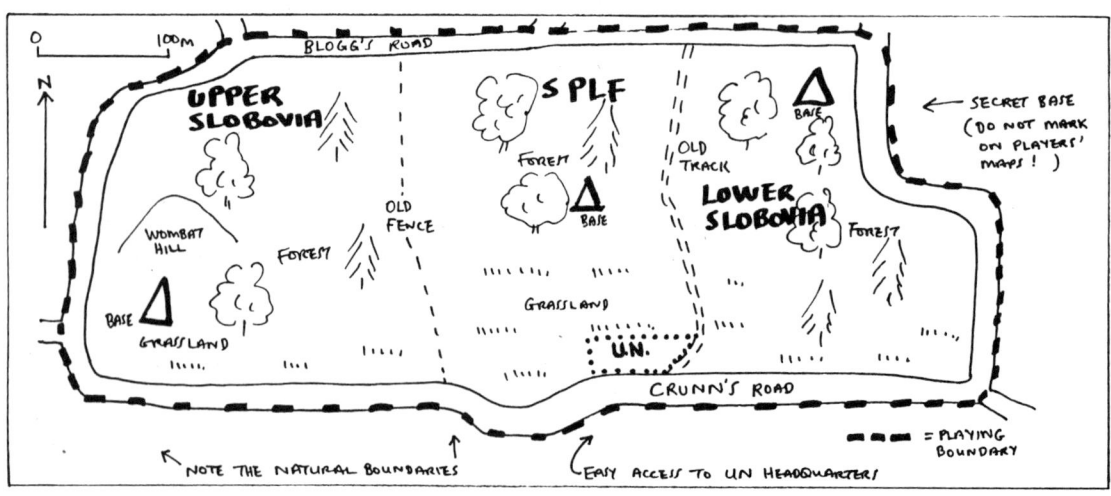

WIDE GAMES

- How can Christians make their message more believable?

Points system

The points system could be as follows:
- Each official box smuggled, pilfered or confiscated is worth the points marked on the label.
- Each tarp/tent pilfered or confiscated is worth 50 points.
- Each trespasser tagged/armband removed is worth 50 points.
- It costs 50 points to collect a 'dead' player from the UN.
- Any breach of time limits involves a loss of 10 points per minute.

VARIATIONS

1 For a more subtle approach, do not mention the word 'country' at all, but present the game as a competition between teams A, B and C. Players will discover the hidden meaning during the de-briefing.

2 Keep the unequal food system a close secret, known only to the UN officials and to you! This makes the game more exciting for the other adults involved.

3 As mentioned in 'Running the activity', normally no team should know what their role is until they are at their secret base. You may prefer to reveal roles much earlier, so that teams can plan their tactics in more detail.

CROSS REFERENCE

For a similar game, see 'Life is not a picnic' earlier in this chapter.

Chapter two
Simulation games

What is a simulation game?
The term is often used in a very general way, but in fact describes a special type of learning activity. Those featured in this chapter are 'games' because they have rules, structures, purpose and often a competitive flavour. The games are designed to 'simulate' or imitate a valuable experience, often one that the players would not normally have. There is almost no limit to the number of experiences that can be simulated. Usually players are given a detailed description of someone from a different time, culture or social class and are asked to imagine themselves living that role. As the game proceeds, they face to various challenges and pressures. They tend to respond to these in an open and honest way because they become totally absorbed by the game.

What makes it so valuable?
In some games the value lies in having the chance to taste another lifestyle. In the safety of an Australian church hall, a youth group could discover what it is like to be the leaders of a persecuted church. This experience might help them to value their Bibles more, or to participate more actively in worship. In other games, the main value comes from reviewing players' performance during the activity. Under pressure, players tend to drop their masks and reveal their strengths and weaknesses—a shy person may reveal great leadership ability, for example, or aggressive behaviour may achieve far less than a humble and co-operative approach Some of these 'lessons' can be predicted because of the structure of a game. Others are a bonus. Either way, they can be very helpful.

Is it risky?
It is true that a poorly-run game can leave players feeling upset and angry. The solution is simple: it is absolutely essential to hold a debriefing at the end of a simulation. (See 'How to debrief' on page 12.) The debriefing process helps players to come out of their game-roles and move back to the real world. It also helps them to express any hurts or anxieties and is an opportunity to examine the main teaching points from the game.

Why use them?
As mentioned above, through simulations, players can have a very valuable experience, one that wouldn't normally be possible. They learn by reflecting on the experience and on their performance; and this leads quite naturally to an exploration of biblical teaching on the theme. For example, the simulation on church persecution mentioned above could be linked to a study of the persecuted church as described in the book of Acts. The final result might be a decision by the players to make better use of the religious freedoms currently available. Whatever the final teaching point, you can be sure that it will be remembered for a long time, because playing the game usually involves intellect, emotions, imagination, and a range of senses. Such involvement helps players to comprehend quite difficult topics and concepts. You will enjoy using these powerful learning tools.

1. Death Angel

10 - 100   1.5 - 2 hours   30 - 900

DESCRIPTION

This dramatic game is designed to show the futility of trying to live without God. Players are encouraged to become absorbed in the materialistic rat-race, and to strive for success. At the end, winners and losers alike get a shock. Death arrives, and levels all, without any respect for power and position. This leads to a discussion about the purpose of life. The message of the Bible is shown to be timeless, true and relevant. Players are challenged to look hard at their own values and beliefs, and to face the fact that they have a limited time on earth.

CHECKLIST

- Matches - allow about one hundred for each person involved.
- Badges and costumes for bank staff, social workers, Death Angels and umpires (see Samples)
- Written instructions for umpires and specialists (above).
- Copies of debriefing questions for discussion leaders (see Samples).
- Sound system for playing music and/or announcements.
- Bibles for all participants.

PREPARATION

1 You will need a hall (a courtyard might also work) with enough space for players to move about in freely. A stage or platform is needed for the 'bank', which should be luxuriously furnished. Along one side of the hall will be the tables and chairs of the 'Social Workers'. An entrance is needed near the stage, for the Death Angels. All of the entrances and exits from the playing area must be temporarily secured and/or guarded at the climax of the game. A public address system may be needed for announcements, and for the playing of background music. Players will each need about 20 matches (or similar) to use in trading.

2 The game requires a Senior Umpire (for announcements, etc), and one extra Umpire for every 15-20 players. All umpires must be thoroughly briefed on the rules and purpose of the game, and should wear badges. They need to be able to give assistance whenever required during playing time. For example, some players may be bewildered, apathetic, or even too excitable. When the game ends, umpires could each lead a discussion group.

3 One Banker is needed for every 40 players. Brief them as follows.

'Your role is to dispense generous loans (in the form of matches) to wealthy clients. You revel in the prestige and power of your position. When the background music stops suddenly, that is your cue to cry out as you catch sight of the sinister Death Angels. As the Death Angels move menacingly towards you, your staff urge you to flee, but you ignore them, trying instead to defend your table with its riches. The Death Angels surround you; you freeze in horror, they touch you and you die, with a hideous scream.'

Each banker needs two security guards, armed with newspaper clubs; and about 30 boxes of matches to loan to wealthy players.

You may also wish to appoint maids and butlers. Brief them as follows.

'You are to welcome and dispense refreshments to wealthy bank clients. When you see the Death Angels approach, you are to cry out a warning to the bankers.'

4 One Social Worker is needed for every 40 players. Each needs a desk, a chair for their own use, a chair for clients and props such as forms, phones, and a box of tissues (to offer clients). They each need a few boxes of matches so that they can give tiny amounts to their needy clients. A large sign should indicate their position in the hall. They need a special briefing before the game.

5 Three Death Angels are needed for every 40 players, with an upper limit of about fifteen. Each needs sinister clothing and make-up. (See Samples.) Brief them as follows.

'You are to move with awesome dignity at all times. Make a grand entrance onto the stage when the background music stops, then slowly close in on the main banking table and surround the bankers. You simply touch the bankers and they die. You then turn menacingly towards the rest of the players and move towards them, exterminating them one by one. When all are 'dead', exit discreetly and change back to normal clothing.'

This role must be done well, or the game becomes a joke. Their arrival on stage is more dramatic if made in silence (the better to hear the screams of the bankers) and followed by loud sinister music (as the Death Angels turn to attack the players). See Samples for ideas on music.

RUNNING THE ACTIVITY

This is how the game might run:

- 1.00 Brief officials and set up hall. Check sound system and finalise props, costumes etc.
- 2.00 Players enter. Explain the game and allow time for questions.
- 2.10 The game begins, with all officials on duty. Matches are issued and trading begins in earnest, using an 'odds & evens' system (see Essential Rules). Play some 'happy' background music.
- 2.20 The first 'wealthy' players begin to appear at the bank, and are pampered with attention and refreshments. They obtain huge loans, and start bankrupting other players. The poor start queuing up to see the social workers. They get lots of advice, a free tissue, and tiny amounts of real help (e.g. three extra matches).
- 2.45 By now the players should be polarised into rich and poor. Before tempers get frayed, prepare your Death Angels to end the game. Give the bankers a subtle signal to be ready.
- 2.50 Stop the background music. The cries of the banking staff will now be heard. Soon all players will freeze and watch the arrival of the sinister Death Angels, who move in on the bankers and surround them. On being touched by the Death Angels, the bankers scream and die. The Death Angels now turn towards the rest of the players.
- 2.55 By now all entrances and exist *must* be guarded and/or secured, because many players will attempt to flee. If you have selected a piece of sinister music, play it at full volume as the Death Angels sweep down upon their victims.
- 3.00 As soon as all players are 'dead', announce that the game is over. The Death Angels withdraw and change. Quickly move players into suitably sized debriefing groups (6-30 people). The designated leaders of these groups can now begin a thorough discussion of the game. See 'How to debrief' on page 12. If leaders signal that they have had enough time, you may want to publicly thank all who have taken part, and to 'officially' close the activity.

ESSENTIAL RULES

1 This is a complex game which must be played by the rules.

2 The Umpires' word is law.

3 All play is to be non-violent.

4 All play is to take place inside the designated playing area.

5 The currency of the game is matches, and you are to seek wealth by 'challenge transactions'. These are initiated by a handshake, which may not be refused. The challenger is to produce a fist closed around a quantity of matches, and to demand that the other player guess whether the amount is 'odd' or 'even' in number. If that person guesses correctly, they get the matches involved. If the guess fails, they must surrender an identical quantity to the challenger. There is no limit to the quantity of matches involved, and there is no need to guess the number of matches. Disputes should go to the umpires.

6 Players are not to form partnerships; they play as individuals.

7 Social Workers are available to care for the poor. Their assessment and level of assistance is final and non-negotiable.

8 Bankers are available to serve players possessing 200 or more matches; free loans of 50 matches will be issued. Bank staff must be obeyed.

9 Should a Death Angel touch you (you will know one when you see one!), you must drop dead on the floor with appropriately hideous screams. Please lie still until instructed to move.

VARIATIONS

1 You may wish to add a dimension of social injustice by setting up inequalities of wealth and privilege. Some players could begin with huge amounts of matches, and/or special legal rights (e.g.

SIMULATION GAMES

limited liability in case of a lost transaction — they pay out only 10 per cent!). If you do this, be sure to explore it carefully in the final debriefing.

2 You can exaggerate the roles of the Bankers and Social Workers to further pursue the idea of social injustice. The Bankers could shower help upon the rich. The Social Workers could be generous with forms and advice, but miserly with matches. Be sure to spend time exploring this theme in post-game discussion.

SAMPLES

Costumes

The more dramatic they are, the better. They could be as follows:
- Social Workers — neat 'Public Service' clothing, badge stating role.
- Bankers — dark suits, tails, tuxedos, etc. Slick hair back, wear a flower on lapel.
- Guards — military clothing, whistles, helmets, and newspaper clubs.
- Death Angels — try to get the 'Grim Reaper' look by making up flowing capes (e.g. from 2 metre squares of black plastic, with central hole for the head), hoods (from matching material in Ku Klux Klan style), and strip-masks to cover the eyes. If you have access to stage make-up, you could consider black hands (with green palms) and black faces (with green vampire fangs, green patches under the eyes). Dark footwear and pants complete the effect. Be aware that for some cultures different colours would be more suitable (e.g. white is the colour of death for some cultural groups).

Music

Music adds atmosphere to the game. Find some bland, happy 'busy' music to accompany trading. Choose from light classical, obsolete pop or commercial radio. Bright lighting will enhance the effect. Switch the music off when the Death Angels appear, and dim the lights to a spotlight on the stage area. Then put on loud, slow, menacing music and turn the amplifier to full volume as the Death Angels turn towards the players in the darkened hall. Good results can be gained by selecting from the following works:
- Holst's *The Planets*, particularly 'Mars'.
- Wagner's 'Ride of the Valkyries'.
- Grieg's *Peer Gynt Suite*, e.g. 'In the Hall of the Mountain King'
- Sibelius' *Finlandia*.

If you can't get these from friends or libraries, try almost any sound track from an adventure film.

Debriefing questions

Even young teens can get into some deep thinking if you use questions (and Bible references) like these. Feel free to push an adult group even harder.
- What was the game about?
- How did you feel during the different stages of the game?
- What aspects of real life does the game illustrate?
- What have you discovered through having played the game?
- Are you a fool if you 'Give up what you cannot keep, in order to gain what you cannot lose?'
- Why did Jesus tell the story of the rich fool? Luke 12:13-21.
- How true to today's world are the verses of Luke 12:29-31?
- Find the two popular proverbs in I Timothy 6:3-10. See also the advice in the subsequent verses (I Timothy 6:17-19).
- What is the effect on the way we live if we really believe that our stay on earth is a short-lived affair?
- What influences distract us from the Christian teachings about life and death?
- What practical choices might help us 'run the race' faithfully, so that we could finally claim II Timothy 4:7 as our own epitaph?

2. Shipwrecked

12 - 60   4 - 24 hours   4 - 40

DESCRIPTION

Many people find that their world is too busy to allow for a hard look at their past, their present or their future. By simulating the enforced idleness of a shipwrecked sailor, this game gives players space to think and allows them to make valuable discoveries. You may vary the precise objectives to meet the needs of your group while retaining the broad aims. In the stillness, there is time and space for players to re-think their faith and the direction their life is taking. This activity can be done on its own, or as part of an expedition or conference. It is often the highlight of an adventure camp.

CHECKLIST

- Printed gear list and worksheets for all participants (see Samples). First-aid kits. Copies of map for leaders.

PREPARATION

1 The first task is to find and inspect a suitable site. What you need is a location where you can tuck people away in complete isolation, but still be able to find them when needed. For safety reasons, it is wise to have an obvious 'freeway' giving access to a number of compact little 'isolation pockets'. A beach provides such a freeway, and there are usually suitable isolation pockets in amongst the dunes and coastal bushland. Likewise, a four-wheel-drive track may link some good pockets of forest. The essential thing is to provide the experience of isolation without sacrificing control and safety. With young teens, you might make the isolation pockets only 50 metres apart. Experienced adults might prefer to be 1000 metres apart, especially if they are in open grassland! If you plan to make regular safety visits on foot, choose thick forest and place people close together.

2 Your next task is to motivate the group to try a somewhat threatening activity. To deal with fears of being alone and being bored, you might read from accounts of famous adventurers, discuss the 'wilderness experiences' of Jesus and other biblical figures, or interview people who have already tried the activity. It may be necessary to start this process some weeks beforehand. The timid and the reluctant may agree to participate only if you guarantee them the right to sleep near a leader.

3 Even with an adult group, it is wise to appoint some leaders. These should be mature and experienced people, able to provide personal counselling as well as first aid. They must be able to ask probing, open-ended questions (see Samples). Each leader is to be in charge of no more than three to five people, and should preferably be of the same sex as their group. If possible, show your leaders the area to be used and even mark out the isolation pockets. Leaders must be placed on the 'freeway' and close to their groups. Discuss possible evacuation routes, safety rules and specific aims; and ensure that leaders fully understand why the activity is being run and how to make it most effective. You may wish to discuss the final debriefing with them so that they can watch for items worthy of group discussion.

4 The equipment required must be as simple as possible. See the list in Samples. You may need to provide some or all of this equipment yourself. Either way, it is wise to issue a gear list well in advance, and to allow time for participants to discuss it with you. An equipment inspection before the activity begins will give leaders a chance to spot faulty (or excess) items.

5 A structured worksheet will help participants make the most of their time as a 'castaway'. If some of your group are exceptionally mature, they may choose

SIMULATION GAMES

to ignore the worksheet. If, however, you target the needs of your group (e.g. marriage, relationships, guilt, spirituality) and give people lots of options to explore, all should be keen to tackle it.

RUNNING THE ACTIVITY

This is how the game might run.

9.00 (am) After breakfast, give a final briefing to all participants. Answer questions, announce departure times and issue extra gear lists as needed.

10.00 Take all leaders on an inspection tour of the playing area. Place markers to indicate where each 'isolation pocket' is, and where each leader will be stationed. Explain first-aid and emergency evacuation procedures clearly. Discuss the possibility of having to cope with wildlife, locals or violent weather.

11.00 Everybody dresses for the activity and packs equipment to be taken. This is the time to monitor the quality and quantity of equipment. Beware of 'heroes' who don't want to take what you know is essential; and of those who lack the ascetic spirit (and plan to bring portable T.V sets, radios, and other unsuitable items.)

12.00 Issue a simple picnic lunch and eat beside the equipment. This is the last chance to note any problems or shortages. There may be some last minute enquiries to be resolved and visits to the toilets.

1.00 Travel to the area. On arrival, explain the safety systems which you plan to use. It might be appropriate to pray as a group before separating. Leaders then head off with their groups to the arranged locations and place each person in their 'pocket'. Campers must know where the leader is to be stationed.

1.30 It may be wise, especially if participants are in earshot of each other, to place a ban on noisy activity after a certain time. You might allow about two hours for any shelter construction or firewood gathering. Fires must never be left unsupervised and their use may be unwise for environmental and safety reasons. Think carefully before allowing them.

3.30 Assuming that the shelter construction is over, participants can rest in their survival shelters. They may have a worksheet to read, a ration pack to explore, or some wildlife to watch. This is the time when they can enjoy the stillness. If leaders plan to do some visiting, make them wait until later. Leaders should be alert for the sound of wanderers during this time, as some participants may already have felt the need to disturb their neighbours. Stop them.

6.00 Meals will be underway by now, and leaders may begin their safety inspections (essential for teenagers). These serve to confirm that participants are coping emotionally and have no urgent needs; and often provide a great opportunity for a deep one-to-one discussion, free from interruption. Leaders must be ready to spend an hour or so if counselling is wanted. Participants who cannot cope with a night out alone should be permitted to move their shelter closer to that of the leader. Seek a compromise so that both retain some isolation and some sense of achievement.

8.00 Participants will probably watch the sunset and then go straight to bed, whatever their age. The leader in charge should move along the 'freeway' in order to check that all is well. The leaders should, of course, be at their pre-arranged location in order to be found.

6.00 (am) Most people will wake with the sun. This is a good time to be alone, so avoid visits if possible. Breakfast takes place.

9.00 A safety visit may be wise around this time, but can be as brief as the situation requires. A long chat may be appropriate if matters from the previous evening need more attention. This is also a good time to explain how you plan to wind things up.

1.00 (pm) Allow each small group to meet and to admire each other's shelters. The group leaders should then ensure that no trace of occupation has been left at the sites. All participants then assemble and return to base. Allow a short amount of time for toilets and a snack. At 2.00 pm move on to the debriefing. (Refer to 'How to debrief' on page 12 for ideas.) Explore how people fared with practical matters, then invite sharing of more personal discoveries. If some participants are reluctant to contribute, respect their privacy. Finish with free time for unpacking, showers, and any further counselling, if needed. It would be a good idea to confer briefly with the leaders, to check that all has gone smoothly.

ESSENTIAL RULES

1 Take only what is on the gear list, no more, no less.

2 Note where your leader is to camp, in case of emergency.

3 Do not stray from your allotted area. You may be needed.

4 Don't disturb others with noise or visits.

5 Be responsible. Build a secure shelter as your first task.

6 Use the whistle call system:

- One blast = nearest leader required, but no one else.
- Two blasts = signal heard, I am coming.
- Three blasts = emergency, all hands needed at once.

7 If you are not coping, consult your leader.

SAMPLES

Menu

This menu works well with teens for a 24-hour 'shipwreck'. For each person provide: 100g salami, 100g dried fruit, 100g cheese, 200g dry biscuits, 200g can fruit, 100g fruit cake, 100g sweets, 100g muesli bars, 125g tin sardines, 100g muesli, powdered milk to make 1/4 litre, tiny Army-style can opener, 30x50cm piece of aluminium foil, fruit drink powder for 1/2L. Note that the foil can be used to make the eating utensils, and that the little can opener may be a puzzler to most teens!

Equipment

With the above menu in mind, you would not put a bowl, mug, spoon or fork on this list, which was designed for Australian summer conditions.
- To wear — Long sleeved shirt, trousers, socks, shoes, hat, pullover, whistle on string, waterproof coat, handkerchief, snake bandage, watch.
- For shelter — Sleeping bag, groundsheet 2mx2m, lilo, string, knife,
- To use — Camera, worksheet, foodpack, insect repellent, Bible, pen, toilet paper, 2 litres water, torch, notepad, small pack to carry it all.

Worksheet

A worksheet might include items like these.
- 'Tuning into the forest' — remove shoes, loosen your clothing, and lie back on your groundsheet. Slow your breathing down until you only need 3 breaths per minute. Note how slow your pulse now is. Start looking around you for different types of plants, and stop when you reach fifty. Now listen for 20 different sounds. Sit up slowly, and sketch the first three moving creatures that you can see. Enjoy the stillness.
- 'Tuning into yourself' — Have the last 12 months been good ones? Why not? Draw a 'happiness graph' of last year. What can you do to make the next 12 months any better? What is the connection between spending time with God, and being happy? How happy are you on a 1-10 scale? What can you do about it?
- 'Tuning into God' — When you are able to be still for an hour, open your Bible to Mark's Gospel. Read it right through non-stop. Now reflect for a moment that Jesus would have done all that, even if you were to be his only convert. Pray quietly, but say the words aloud, as if to someone beside you. Praise Jesus for his courage, love and patience. Then describe the ten people who love you the most, and thank God for them. Close off by asking the Spirit to steer you through the next year's adventures.

Questions

When visiting a person on a 'Shipwreck' exercise, avoid questions which can be answered with a 'yes/no' response. Clumsy intrusive questions (e.g. What are your problems?) may cause the hearer to clam up. Here are some useful open-ended questions which encourage the hearer to respond.
- How are you coping with being alone?
- What did you think of the worksheet?
- How do you feel when you read the Bible by yourself?
- Where do you rate on a 'happiness scale' of 1-10?
- If you had 10 minutes on the phone to God, what would you ask him?
- What do you find hardest about being a teenager/Christian/atheist?
- What do you like/dislike about yourself?
- What has been your spiritual highlight in the last 12 months?
- Do people understand who you really are, or who you want to be?
- What control do you have over who you will be in 10 years time?

VARIATIONS

1 Half a day alone is enough for the average 12 year old.

2 An overnight experience is too stressful for ages 12-15. They could be alone until dusk, and then be allowed to share a tent with others.

3 Ages 16-18 generally find 24 hours to be all that they can enjoy.

4 Mature young adults may be ready for 2-3 days alone, if you prepare them through some shorter experiences first.

5 The degree of stress and challenge can be varied by controlling the quantity and quality of food, equipment, clothing etc. The location and season can also make a big difference as can variations in the acuteness of the worksheet questions.

3. Sell it if you can

15 - 100 | 2 - 3 hours | 40 - 120

DESCRIPTION

This complex game appears to focus on communication skills, and to relate them to advertising. Players will initially see little more in it than that, as they busily prepare advertising campaigns. Only as the game ends do they discover that it is really an exploration of some different approaches to evangelism. It is both humbling and exciting to discover that one of the best ways to share the gospel is to spend time talking with people.

CHECKLIST

- Resources for each advertising team: one tape recorder (prepared for recording), a big carton (or video camera and playback gear), large sheets of white paper, paints and brushes, crayons and textas, scissors, sticky tape.
- Copies of audience roles and advertising campaign instructions for players and umpires (see Samples)
- Ballot slips for the audience team
- Copies of roles for players and umpires
- Bibles, pens and paper for all participants.

PREPARATION

1 Umpires are needed to keep the game moving smoothly. Appoint one umpire for every 10-12 players, and explain the game thoroughly to them. They will need a printed copy of the rules, small-group roles, and likely time-schedule. One umpire must act as a chairperson in the final debriefing, controlling questions and debate.

2 Divide players into two even-sized teams and split up each of these teams into small groups of six players. (See Variations.)

3 Audience team members will each need a ballot slip bearing a list of all products advertised during the game (see point 7 below). The list must allow them to rank products by writing a number beside each entry. You may need to appoint poll clerks to issue the ballot slips to players, and to count votes at the end of the game. Allow for one poll clerk per 30 players.

4 The advertising campaigns require the resources mentioned in the checklist.

5 You will need one large hall (big enough for all to move about in) plus another hall (or some smaller rooms). In the large hall, place clusters of chairs so that two groups can be seated in each cluster (e.g. if groups contain six players each, then twelve chairs are needed per cluster. One row of six chairs should face the other row of six, with two metres separating the rows). When the game is fully underway, all players will be using the large hall. During the early phase, those preparing advertising material will use the other hall (or small rooms). A public address system in the large hall would be an advantage.

6 Prepare role cards for the audience teams (see Samples).

7 Prepare campaign instructions for the advertising teams, featuring the products and methods shown in Samples.

RUNNING THE ACTIVITY

This is how the game might run:
- 1.00 Assemble all poll clerks, umpires, instruction sheets and resource materials. Give a detailed final briefing on the game, and allow time for questions. Then prepare the rooms to be used for the game.

2.00 Call in all players and officials, and explain the basic rules. Deal with any questions, and then split the group into two teams of even size, according to your prepared plan. The 'Audience Team' go to the large hall to be briefed on their roles. The 'Advertising Team' go to the other rooms where their resources, and a briefing, await them.

2.20 The Audience team can now be placed in their small groups and given their role cards. They will need time to think about their roles and to prepare for a practice run, in which they listen to an umpire give a persuasive talk (for 1 minute) on the virtues of 'garlic aftershave' (or similar). As each group has its 'practice run', the others should watch closely; they may then offer constructive criticism to help the group express their role clearly (e.g. as a very aggressive audience). Meanwhile, form the Advertising team into small groups, and issue the groups with their campaign instructions. Give these groups 20-30 minutes to prepare a 3-minute presentation for their product. Tell them that they will need to repeat this presentation a number of times to small audiences.

2.50 If one team is prepared well before the other, encourage a discussion on 'body language', 'ethics in advertising' or 'effective sales methods'.

3.00 The game now begins in earnest in the large hall. Each Audience group sits together, facing the empty chairs reserved for the Advertising group. The umpires then bring in the Advertising Team, and each advertising group chooses an audience group. At a signal, the Advertising groups begin their presentations, stopping after 3 minutes at another signal. After a brief rest, the Advertising teams move clockwise to their next audience and repeat their presentations. The cycle continues until each advertising group has performed to each audience group.

3.30 When the cycle has been completed, the Advertisers withdraw in their small groups to discuss the different audiences they faced. Each group should then appoint a spokesperson to present a report (at the final debriefing) on the first and last audiences they faced. Groups have 10 minutes to prepare this report. Meanwhile, issue each member of the Audience team with a ballot and ask them to complete it without comment. They will have one minute to rank the products advertised in order of preference i.e. (1) for the product they would first buy, (2) for the second, and so on. The Poll Clerks collect and count the voting slips while the Audience groups meet for 10 minutes to decide as groups which was the most effective advertising campaign. If time allows they could rank all the campaigns in order of effectiveness. The next 8 minutes should be spent in helping a spokesperson for each group prepare a report on the second advertising campaign they received.

3.55 Both teams now gather in the large hall for the final debriefing. See 'How to debrief' on page 12. Audience and Advertising groups present their reports. The voting process could be discussed and the Poll Clerks could present the results of voting for comment.

4.20 The scene is now set to explore the similarities between selling a product and presenting the gospel (See Samples for questions and Bible references.) The validity of using modern media to evangelise could also be discussed. Some players might have experienced 'audience responses' similar to those of the game when engaged in evangelism. Discuss how Christians can cope with responses like apathy, hostility or interest, and gather ideas on other ways which Christians could use to present the faith. Close with worship and prayer.

ESSENTIAL RULES

1 The Umpires' word is law.
2 Follow written instructions carefully.
3 During the advertising presentations The Audience groups must sit on a row of chairs which faces the row to be used by the visitors. The Audience must stay seated, but may choose to look away. The Advertisers may move about at will.

SAMPLES

Audience roles

- Aggressive individuals — disagree strongly, no teamwork.
- Aggressive collaborators — disagree strongly, but a close team.
- Apathetic individuals — (yawn), no interest, no teamwork.
- Apathetic collaborators — no interest, but a close team (smug clique).
- Interested individuals — curious and keen, no teamwork.
- Interested collaborators — curious and keen, but a close team.

Advertising campaign instructions

- One to one talkers—selling 'Joy Gargle Mouthwash' (the breath that leaves lovers breathless).

SIMULATION GAMES

- T.V. advertisers — selling 'Twinkle Toes Foot Talc' ('Don't be defeated, make him toe the line.') Video recording and playback equipment is ideal, but it works just as well if actors' heads appear inside a cardboard carton (modified to resemble a T.V. set).
- Radio advertisers — selling 'Mother Nature Health Soap' (Get rid of those underarm smellies.) Cassette recording gear is ideal, but an improvised arrangement with voices singing behind a screen will do the job.
- Poster makers — selling 'Glowing Curls Hair Restorer' (Take dandruff out of your life, and let a new man in). Paper, paints, etc.
- Public speakers — selling 'Solar Block Salve'. (Surfside kisses last up to 37 per cent longer.)
- Poster writers — selling 'Hollywood Smile Toothpaste' (A denture adventure for a rising star). Poster gear, but without any illustrations.

Questions
Questions for the final debrief could include:
- Should the Christian faith be 'sold' as if it was toothpaste?
- Where does the Bible say that we should share our faith? (Acts 1:8)
- Should an ancient faith use the modern electronic media?
- Were the responses of the Audience team true to real life?
- Do 'results' justify using any means to gather converts?
- How can Christians make their message more believable?

Bible references
Bible references to consider are:
- Colossians 4:3-6; Acts 2:42-47, 5:11-16, 5:42, 17:16-34; II Timothy 1:6-8, 4:2-5; Luke 12:8-9, 24:47.
- See Leviticus chapters 19 and 26 for examples of lifestyle evangelism.

VARIATIONS

1 Where total playing numbers are small, use groups of 4-5 players and include three or four groups on each team. Ensure that one group uses the 'one to one talking' method.

2 If numbers are large, do not exceed 6-8 players in each group. Use up to seven groups per team — beyond this, total confusion will set in. It would be better to split into two or more completely separate games. Perfect numbers are 6 groups of 6 players per team i.e. a total of 72 players.

4. The politicians

15 - 100   1.5 - 2 hours   15 - 50

DESCRIPTION

A small group of politicians meet some aggressive lobby groups and find that pleasing everyone is not easy! This game helps players to come to grips with the reality of politics, whether at a national level or in a local church. The game is also a lesson in Christian leadership, as players must choose between idealism and pragmatism. By the finish, players should be willing to show more tolerance and support for those in leadership positions; and they will have looked into the fascinating world of Christian ethics. The concluding Bible exploration should help players realise that biblical leaders often faced difficult decisions and that 'politics' is part of the process of living in a community. The game is fairly stressful, especially for those playing the politicians.

CHECKLIST

- Copies of instructions, roles and rules for umpires.
- Copies of roles for each team.
- Bibles for all participants.

PREPARATION

1 The playing area should include a space large enough to seat the whole group for the final debriefing. When the game is underway, the politicians (four or more people) will each need their own room, out of hearing range of the others.

2 You will need umpires to monitor the performance of each politician and each lobby group. Umpires must be fully briefed on the rules, time schedule and aims of the activity.

3 Select five teams. Four of these teams will be lobby groups of equal size and each of them should include a couple of fairly confident and alert players. The fifth team are the 'politicians', and must include four or more players. They have a rather demanding role, so choose reasonably articulate people who are blessed with robust egos.

4 Teams will need a written description of their roles and copies of the essential rules.

RUNNING THE ACTIVITY

This is how the game might run:

1.00 Assemble all players. Give a summary of the game, read out the rules, announce teams, issue roles and send them off (with their umpires) to prepare.

1.10 Allow time for teams to study the rules and roles and plan tactics. The roles for each of the five groups should be treated as 'top secret', and should not be made available to rivals.

1.30 Check that all players are ready, then place the politicians in four separate rooms. They are not to communicate with each other.

1.35 At a signal, umpires take each lobby group to one of the politicians and discussion begins. Lobby groups may wish to employ different spokespersons during the game. If the politicians are working in pairs, they could take it in turns to be the 'active' member.

1.45 Another signal will close the discussion. Politicians stay put and umpires lead their teams to the next politician on their schedule.

1.55 This pattern continues without any breaks until each lobby group has met each politician.

2.15 With all four cycles completed, allow the five groups to relax for a few minutes. Then call

SIMULATION GAMES

everyone together for the debriefing. (See 'How to debrief' on page 12.) In the debrief, be sure to expose any lies, contradictions, and broken promises from the politicians. This is best done by debriefing each lobby group in turn, and then the politicians. You might put the politicians 'on trial', allowing the lobby groups to cross-examine them. The discussion then moves to an exploration of the hard realities of politics which you could relate to the 'politics' operating in any group of people. The group could reflect on difficult choices faced by their current church leadership. Allow 45 minutes for this part of the discussion. Finally, explore some Bible verses. (See Samples.) Close off by praying for those in power at local and national levels.

ESSENTIAL RULES

1 Teams must follow their roles and instructions carefully.

2 The Umpires' word is law.

3 Once the game has started, the politicians may not communicate with each other, nor may any communication take place between the different lobby groups.

SAMPLES

Discussion questions

These look at general issues.
- How important is the need to get votes to stay in power?
- Why are selfish single-issue lobbyists such a problem for politicians?
- Why is it sometimes so hard to find the most ethical option?
- Why is it sometimes so difficult for leaders to keep every promise they make?

Bible passages

These relate to political activity.
See Acts 11:1-18, Acts 15:1-21 and Galatians 2:11-14 for accounts of early church politics concerning Gentile admission.
- For a lesson in sheer courage, read about Nathan's actions in II Samuel, chapters 11 and 12. See also the account of John the Baptist's death in Matthew 14:1-12.
- For complexity, look at another prophet's situation in Jeremiah 38. Look at the Christian leadership qualities listed in I Timothy 3: 1-13.
Consider the long-term political implications for slavery of Philemon 1:16, and reflect on the long battle by Christians to abolish the slave trade.

Role cards

Two sets are provided below. The first ones relate to a dispute inside a local church, where the elders take the role of the Politicians.

(A) Social Committee

You are all members of the Church Social Committee, and for the last 75 years have run a prestigious, fund-raising debutante ball. You feel strongly that Christians should be able to have fun — and there has never been any problem with drunks or fights. Indicate that if the 'killjoys' get their way, your whole committee will resign and join the church down the road. Remind the elders that the ball makes over $15,000 from champagne sales alone, with ticket sales producing around $15,000 after expenses. Make the Elders promise that the event will continue.

(B) Building Appeal Committee

You are all long-term members of the Church Building Appeal Committee, and want to see the youth ministry centre built as soon as possible. Remind the elders that you have a very competitive quote from a Christian builder, and that you are within $20,000 of having sufficient funds to begin work. You might add that the centre was due to be finished by now, and that the youth group desperately needs room to meet. Make it clear that you want the money and the authority to get work underway this year.

(C) Temperance League

You are all members of the church branch of the National Temperance League, whose Central Committee has recently challenged you to show more determination and courage in your fight against alcohol. The debutante ball is your priority target, because of the volume of liquor consumed and also because of the ball's high profile. Tell the elders that the Church needs to set an example to the whole community, and that banning of alcohol from the ball is a vital first step. Remind them of the problems associated with alcoholism and demand an assurance that all church functions will be teetotal in future.

(D) Church Elders

You are all elders of a very active suburban church which has a high local profile because of its well-run social events. Because of them, membership has doubled over the last ten years. The youth work is booming, with about 140 youngsters involved. The cost of supporting a large pastoral team has made it difficult to balance the budget, but you hope to build a new youth ministry centre in the near future. You are proud of the unity within the membership, and of the number of lively ministries in the Church.

(E) Youth board

You supervise the work of two full-time Youth Pastors and provide support for about 40 voluntary helpers. The two Pastors and volunteers have put enormous pressure on you to build the youth ministry centre this year. It the elders do not agree to this, you may have to cope with a wave of resignations. The situation is desperate.

The second set of roles relate to state or national politics.

(F) The Politicians

You are all members of the 'Christian Reform party' and are committed to the following policies.
- Society will be drug-free within 10 years (no tobacco, alcohol, etc).
- Taxes will be lowered over the next 10 years. The party must win four more seats in the coming election, or it will lose power and be unable to bring in its policies.

(G) The Save Our Youth League

You are a powerful lobby group with an uncompromising anti-drugs stance. Greet each politician with great warmth, ask for their health policy, and explain your position. Conclude by demanding an assurance that the tobacco trade will soon be a thing of the past and that tobacco advertising will be banned by the end of the year.

(H) The Christian Farmers Fellowship

You are to demand assistance for struggling small primary producers, pointing out that your region grows crops for export. Ask the politicians for their health policy (just in case it opposes tobacco). Finally, reveal that all your equipment and buildings are geared to tobacco production. You might (reluctantly) agree to change to less lucrative crops if generous financial assistance is available.

(I) The Sporting Union

You thank each politician for the generous annual grants, which are based on the tobacco tax. Point out that this tax pays for your clubhouses, changing rooms, staffing, ovals and uniforms and that spectator facilities are provided by tobacco sponsors. Ask the politicians to explain their party's sport and health policies, and demand a promise that sport will continue to get favourable treatment.

(J) The Tax Cuts Now Group

You explain that families and businesses are over-taxed. You offer your considerable voting power if given detailed assurances that Government subsidies and grants will be severely pruned. You all believe in low taxes and minimal intervention by Government.

VARIATIONS

1 The game works quite well with only three lobby groups. If this is preferred, reduce the politicians to three individuals (or three pairs).

2 For maximum participation and enjoyment, the game should not involve more than fifty players. If you have large numbers, run two or more smaller games at the same time.

3 You can devise role cards to suit the exact needs of your group. For example, it would take little effort to portray a dispute over the job description for the new assistant pastor. The Social Concern Group, Youth Group, Senior Citizens, and Young Mothers could all have fixed ideas on how this person's time should be spent.

5. 1984

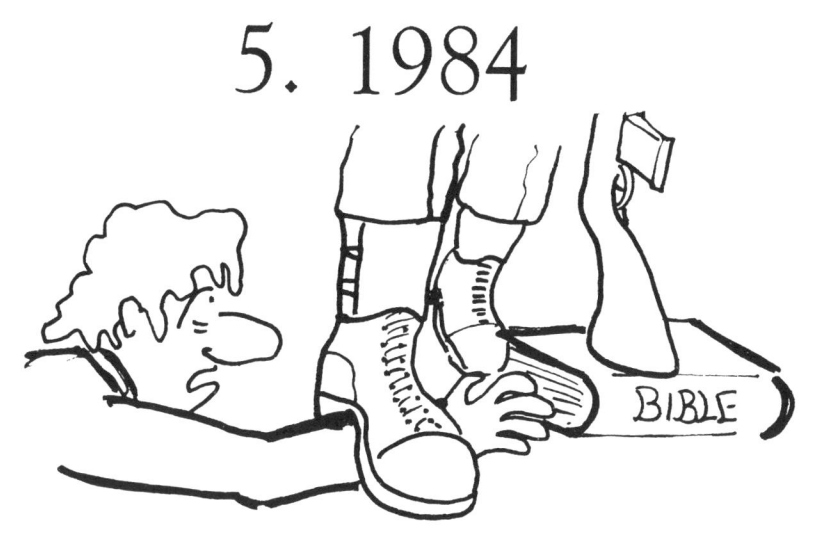

DESCRIPTION

Inspired by George Orwell's chilling novel of the same name, '1984' is an exciting, stressful and thought-provoking experience. Through playing '1984', participants come to understand what it is like to lose one's religious freedoms and to be persecuted. The game helps them to clarify their faith and to value it more; and drives home the importance of the Bible. It shows that true discipleship involves courage, risk-taking and close teamwork. '1984' is best played at night. Sinister 'Secret Police' do all in their power to stop the 'Thought Criminals' (Christians) from retaining and expanding their illegal stocks of Scripture materials. The game climaxes with a heroic smuggling run to a waiting courier.

CHECKLIST

- A role card, copy of rules and points system for each team (see Samples)
- Map of playing area for each team
- Written instructions, and items listed above, for umpires and couriers.
- Matches and candles.
- Costumes and equipment for Police and Criminals.

PREPARATION

1 Inspect the playing area carefully. You need a number of small rooms for the Thought Criminals, and a large central room for the Police. Remove or secure any fragile items in these rooms, and ensure that people are able to move safely from room to room in the dark. The closing phase requires a safe, open area which gives access to a boundary fence where the courier will wait. Produce a map of the playing area so that everybody knows the boundaries. Some buildings and zones may need to be declared 'out of bounds'.

2 Choose teams and produce copies of roles, rules, points, times, etc. The four key groups in the game are as follows:

- The Umpires — need a uniform (e.g. white shirt), watches, copies of all rules and points systems, map, role cards, written instructions, pen and pad for adding up point scores, and a careful briefing. One umpire will be attached to the Police, the Head Umpire will roam freely, and the remainder will each be attached to one room of Criminals. Those in rooms with Criminals need a supply of 'Visa Slips' (e.g. one per criminal). Arrange a clear system for handling first aid or other emergencies.
- The Secret Police — use about 15 per cent of the players for this group, choosing the taller and more mature members. Imaginative use of sinister clothing and even make-up is encouraged. They also need symbolic weapons (e.g. clubs, holsters) and powerful torches. You may need to 'train' this group in the arts of (non-violent) aggressive intimidation, and of searching for forbidden stockpiles of Bibles etc. A detailed briefing is essential. Only the Umpires may know who is in this group — the secrecy adds drama.
- The Courier — one or two reliable people are needed to arrive very furtively at the secret rendezvous point to collect Bible materials. They must dress as spies and carry briefcases (or similar). An accurate watch is vital, because the courier is only to wait for 10 seconds at the edge of the playing area. Why not use a fast, dark car?
- The Thought Criminals — use all remaining players and adults for this group, but instruct adults to avoid taking on leadership. Assign

teams of four to ten players to each room used. A copy of the rules should be issued to each team. You may wish to conceal matches and a candle in each room. Criminals will need Bibles, pens, and paper. They will need some time to plan tactics together, but require no special briefing. They will be present at the start of the game when it is explained to everybody.

RUNNING THE ACTIVITY

This is how the game might run:

The day before

Give a description of the game to all players. Appoint and brief umpires, Courier, and Police. Ensure that the identity of the Police is kept secret. Check that necessary props and costumes are available.

On the day

1.00(pm) Give a full explanation of the game to the whole group, but do not announce teams. This second briefing may take up to an hour because players will have lots of questions. When players seem to be clear about the rules and purpose of the game, finish the briefing and run your afternoon program. Final preparations may be completed, including the hiding of candles and matches in rooms to be used by the Thought Criminals.

7.00 Final briefing to all. Synchronise watches. Announce teams, sending Criminals to their rooms accompanied by their umpires. Police then move to their headquarters. Umpires explain rules, roles, points, boundaries etc. and show the criminals how to respond to a Police raid (with terrified respect and obedience). Criminals plan tactics, and clear rooms of fragile, personal or unwanted items. Police put on their uniforms, organise their room, and practice being aggressive.

7.50 Amnesty period. Nervous Criminals are permitted to send one messenger per room to the umpire outside the Police headquarters, to hand in Bibles (thus losing points per Bible).

7.55 All Criminals must be back in their rooms.

8.00 Bell or horn announces start of game. Criminals may begin writing out pages of Scripture by candlelight as per the rules. Police are seen for the first time, as they begin their raids and patrols. Criminals use 'Visas' to visit other criminals or to pilfer Bibles from the Police headquarters.

8.30 One (or more) umpires reveal the time and location of the Courier to their rooms of Criminals. Criminals attempt to relay this information to all the rooms. (Deliveries to the courier earn big point scores.)

8.40 Courier discreetly moves into position, without revealing time or location to the Police. Criminals prepare for the big moment.

8.58 Courier appears at the set location, waits for 10 seconds only, then makes rapid exit. By staying outside the playing boundary, the courier is safe from arrest. Meanwhile the Police pursue those Criminals involved in the Bible pick-up.

9.00 Bell, or horn, announces the end of play. Players remove any costumes and all gather for a careful debriefing. (See 'How to debrief' on page 12.) While this is getting underway, the Courier and Umpires should add up the points scores (for Police, each Criminal room, Criminal total) so that they can be announced. The debriefing may include a couple of short readings about twentieth century Christians under persecution. When the debriefing is completed, provide supper and time for relaxation. If appropriate, restore rooms used to their normal state. Umpires should be especially alert for players who are upset as a result of the game. For example, two friends may be unable to relate normally, because the game placed them on opposing sides. Typically, the 'victim' has to be assured that the friendship continues, and that the role-playing is all over. This applies to adults as much as to teenagers.

ESSENTIAL RULES

1 The Umpires' word is law.

2 The game is to be non-violent and property must not be harmed.

3 All play is to be inside the set boundaries and time-limits.

4 The Criminals -

- May not leave their room without a 'Visa Slip'. If tagged by Police outside their room, must stop and surrender their Visa, and any Scripture materials they have.
- Once tagged, return directly to their room, without any involvement in the game until back inside the room.
- May enter other Criminal rooms, but are not 'safe' there.
- May pilfer Scripture materials from the police headquarters, if they dare.
- May only conceal Scripture materials in one of the Criminal rooms.
- May smuggle items to other Criminal rooms or to the Courier.
- May not conceal Scripture materials on their

SIMULATION GAMES

person.
- Must respectfully obey all Police orders to sit, stand, etc. (when inside a room.)

5 The Police -
- May not raid a room unless 40 per cent of all Police are present.
- May not stay longer than 10 minutes at a time in any one room.
- Must take confiscated Scripture materials directly to the Police headquarters, and place it on a central table or chair in full view. (The same applies to material handed in voluntarily.)

SAMPLES

Point scores

These could be as follows for Criminals:
- 1 point loss per Bible handed in before play begins.
- 5 point loss per complete/incomplete page of Scripture found by Police.
- 10 point loss per Bible found by Police.
- 10 point loss for any Visa taken after Police tag a Criminal.
- 20 points gained for any page of 100 words of recognisable biblical material (e.g. accounts of biblical events) given to Courier.
- 30 points gained for any page of 100 words of accurately copied or memorised biblical text (with book, chapter, verse) given to Courier.
- 100 points gained per Bible smuggled to Courier.

Role cards

These could be as follows.

Secret Police
- You are the dreaded Secret Police, with enormous powers.
- You must keep your identity secret until the game starts.
- You need a sinister uniform, a symbolic weapon, and a powerful torch. A very loud whistle may be useful.
- Your task is to guard your stockpile of Scripture materials, to prevent smuggling of such materials, to catch any criminals who are outside their proper rooms, and to prevent the storage/production of Scripture materials in the rooms of the Criminals. Note the points system, the times of play, and the essential rules. When raiding a room, intimidate the Criminals by shouting, blowing whistles loudly, shining torches into faces, etc. Make them lie face down as you search. You may only confiscate items listed in the points system. Watch for signs of a Courier coming to collect Scripture material.

Thought Criminals
- Your religious thoughts are offensive to the Secret Police.
- They have absolute power to raid your room, order you about and confiscate any printed or handwritten Scripture material.
- You must meekly obey their orders.
- Note the points system, the times of play, and the essential rules.
- Your umpire may not lead, but will co-operate with you in the production of Scripture material.
- If you lose your lights, look for a concealed candle and matches.
- Your Visa supply is limited to one per criminal. Remember the Courier!
- Be clever, or all your Bibles will be found in the first raid.
- Help your fellow Thought Criminals as much as you can.

VARIATIONS

1 If numbers exceed the suggested limit of 50, split up the group and run a number of games. This simulation involves a lot of pressure and stress, and for this reason numbers playing each game should be kept low.

2 For more complexity, plant spies in each room of Criminals. Appoint and brief spies well before the game is announced, doing this as subtly as possible (e.g. by secret note). Spies try to slip information to the Police (who do not know their identity), and if detected by the Criminals, must join the Police. A majority vote by the group will decide on such an expulsion. Criminals who are wrongly declared to be 'Spies' by their groups must also join the Police. Umpires are to warn their groups of the existence of spies once the game has been underway for 15 minutes.

3 If a 'wide game' flavour is desired, you could adjust the number of Couriers and the size of the playing area. A wonderfully complex finale is guaranteed if a few Couriers call at staggered times over acres of bushland. Some additional rules would be needed for safety e.g. the presence of umpires with each group of smugglers. Such variations do not lessen the need for a thorough debriefing after the game.

4 For added emotional stress, set up some scenes of bribery and betrayal. Criminals could infuriate their colleagues by publicly accepting a Police bribe, revealing the location of hidden materials, and then exiting with the Police. Remember though that many adults find this game painfully intense as it is.

First law of christian education
'Enthusiasm covers a multitude of sins and omissions.'

The costumes may be a little tired, the cassette player near death, and the temperature around 50 degrees celsius, but a dose of enthusiasm can carry the day. Conversely, the most superbly planned activity can be like chloroform if the leaders don't have the desire to make it go. Show good-humoured determination to make the activity really 'fire', and it usually will. The ideal combination, however, is enthusiasm *and* very careful planning for every possible contingency.

Second law of christian education
'The 3 secrets of smooth present-ation are prepar-ation, preparation and preparation.'

The well prepared group leader can face almost any problem with a serenely inscrutable smile.
Why? — because she has resources and plans to cope with setbacks. You should allow for the odd power failure, heavy downpour, lost child, late bus or deranged bull-elephant. The simplicity and smoothness of some programs is deceptive; things look simple only because a huge amount of preparation has been done. If a problem arises, all that is needed is a smooth change to a different gear.

Third law of christian education
'A thing worth starting is worth finishing.'

Imagine taking a group of excited kids to the front gate of Disneyland, and then not going inside! It is just as frustrating when leaders put their group through a simulation or role play and fail to conclude with a debriefing. Know what your big teaching point is, and then drive it home! The activity is then satisfyingly complete for all concerned. This does not stop you from waiting for a deliberate period before explaining a hidden teaching point. Mystery is fun.

Chapter three
Role-plays

What exactly is a role-play?
If you take part in a role play you will not receive pages of dialogue to memorise. You will simply be given an identity (or 'role'), and asked to behave according to that identity in a simple scene. For example, you might be told to take on the role of an angry shopkeeper who has caught a child stealing sweets. You might also be told that the scene will involve certain other people, or that it should end in a particular way. Your instruction might read as follows.

'The scene involves the guilty child, the angry shopkeeper, a policeman, and the wealthy parent of the child. The shopkeeper catches the child in the act, calls the policeman, and is about to demand prosecution. The parent suddenly arrives, and after a few minutes the problem is resolved to everyone's satisfaction.'

Note that there is considerable room for creative initiative. Players can try hard to act out their roles consistently, and to seek a resolution of the conflict.

Why not have a detailed script?
In a script, most of the action and emotion is decided by the author. Some people find it difficult to learn a script. In contrast, a typical role, such as the one above, takes only a minute to absorb and the player's own personality is the main force, guided by the given role description. The resulting spontaneity is exciting—no-one can predict exactly how a role-play will run. Audiences often find a role-play makes compelling viewing, because of its 'true to life' flavour.

Why are role-plays valued so highly?
Acting out a role forces a person to 'live in someone else's shoes' for a few minutes. This can be a powerful and valuable experience—it enables them to understand the emotions, motives and culture of another person. Self-discovery is also involved: players learn about themselves and their ability to cope with certain situations. The example mentioned earlier might help you (as the shopkeeper) discover a harsh and unforgiving streak in your personality! Role-plays are also an excellent training tool. The lessons are convincing and long remembered. If you need to train your youth leaders in the art of conflict resolution, design some appropriate role-plays. Perhaps your church elders can't imagine what it is like to be teased for being a Christian. Do your teenagers understand why their parents are so strict? The process of role-playing some suitable scenes tends to arouse interest by getting brains and emotions into gear. Next comes a discussion, further teaching and Bible exploration to complete the learning process.

Make sure it works
Role-plays can be a flop. To avoid problems, firstly have a warm up session to help people relax. Secondly, choose players wisely. Pick natural 'hams' for the first couple of scenes if you can, and don't give people roles which they might find unpleasant and stressful. Finally, remember to debrief sensitively, watching for clues that anyone has been upset. If you find a problem, act at once, either in the group or privately.

How to warm up your group
Because so many people feel shy or inadequate about performing in public, you will need to create a warm, supportive atmosphere in the group. Once those present feel relaxed, and have had a friendly laugh at each other, you can begin the role-plays proper. Below are some sample warm up activities for you to try. Later you will feel able to create your own.

Example one
These were used to warm up a group of sixty strangers. Teams of ten were formed, and each given several 5-minute roles to play. For example:
- Form a human pyramid by getting down on all fours, placing four people on the first layer, three on the next etc. Once you are all 'up', challenge the tug-of-war team to form an identical pyramid and to race you over a 3 metre course.
- Find the big white rope and prepare for a tug-of-war. Find the pyramid group and challenge them to a tug.
- You are a wolf pack. Move about, snarling and howling in a terrifying manner. Attack the flock of sheep and try to collect all of their shoes, socks, sandals, etc. Beware of being dragged into the circle of sheep, because you must then play dead.
- You are a flock of sheep. Sit on the floor in a tight circle, bleating loudly, especially if wolves approach. They will try to take your footwear, and you must prevent them.
- Form a political meeting in the middle of the room. Stand in an adoring circle around your speaker who will urge you to support 'Land rights for gay whales', or something equally silly. Encourage your speaker with very noisy cheers, applause, 'Hear hears', etc.
- Form the shape of a large elephant, and plod around the room with trunk swaying. Sing majestic old hymns, and pause beside the political meeting to shout 'What about the workers?'

At the end of each 5-minute round, rotate roles, so that each of the six teams plays a number of different ones.

Example two
This example was used to warm-up a group of twenty young adults from one church. Two even-sized teams were formed, and the competition began. An umpire called for a volunteer from each team to come forward and sit in the centre of the circle. These competitors sat facing each other, with knees almost touching. They were each given different (crazy) topics to speak on, had 20 seconds to prepare, and then, speaking at the same time, had to harangue each other for 30 seconds. The one stopping or laughing first would be the loser. The results were very entertaining, the final points score being of minor importance. Once the first two volunteers had performed, all other team members were encouraged to take a turn. Some of the topics were:
- The price of fish in Northern China.
- A short history of the world.
- The sex-life of mushrooms.
- The difference between ducks.
- Why aardvarks never vote for Marxist politicians.
- The first law of thermo-dynamics.
- Why Shakespeare's plays have never been translated into Swahili.

At the end of all this, the group was ready to tackle any role-play.

How to control the process
Because role-plays are a powerful learning tool, they must be kept under control. If a scene is drifting off track, intervene. Role-plays are not meant to be 'program fillers', but aids to learning. Know what you are trying to teach; choose or create the most appropriate scenes; and stop the acting when it has clearly made its point. Leave ample time for de-briefing, teaching, Bible exploration and discussion—if the action has been hot, the group needs to cool down.

How to 'cool down' your group
Unlike simulations or wide games, which can run for hours, role-plays are usually over in a few minutes. Because the emotions generated can be so intense, however, the same care in de-briefing is required. Don't let more than two or three items take place without calling a halt and having a detailed post-mortem. To return to the example given earlier (with an irate shopkeeper, young thief, etc.), you might run the de-briefing like this.
- Announce that the scene is over and return participants to their seats.
- Ask the audience to comment on the various phases of the scene. Explore each in turn, paying attention to the key teaching points (such as the willingness to forgive, to apologise, to repent, etc). Ask if the action seemed true to life, and if a small change might have led to a very different conclusion.
- Ask the actors to share their feelings, especially if they seemed to immerse themselves in their roles. Help them to 'step out' of their roles and to look back at what took place. For example, the 'child' (in the scene mentioned earlier) might feel hurt that their apology was swept aside by the angry shopkeeper. You would deal with such hurts by reassuring the 'victim' that the scene is all over, and that they are loved.
- If it becomes apparent that the role-play failed to illustrate the teaching point properly, do a re-run with the same, or different, actors, then de-brief again.
- Move on to the next set of role-plays, or close the session with some appropriate teaching on the topic. If the group is a bit tense, wind things down with some gentle singing and worship. Give people time to relax further over supper.

1. Faith sharing

10 - 100   1 - 2 hours   6 - 600

DESCRIPTION

This activity is designed to help Christians who have little experience in talking about their faith in a natural and relaxed manner. Participants take turns at playing three roles: an observer; an interviewer who poses a series of questions about the Christian faith; and an interviewee. This simple process of talking about one's faith helps Christians to clarify their beliefs and equips them to explain their faith to others in a style that is jargon free and avoids embarrassment. The questions are graded so that everybody can participate comfortably in the early stages, whatever their level of Christian experience. The first question is 'Who was Jesus?' while the later ones challenge the speaker to spell out current beliefs and their impact on daily life. As the session progresses, players who have confused beliefs may begin to feel uncomfortable; they could be allowed to sit back and act as observers if they wish.

CHECKLIST

- Copies of rules and questions for each group (see Samples)
- Printed resources and a Bible for each participant.

PREPARATION

1 The Samples section has questions to suit a wide age-range. If you wish to prepare your own, first discuss the precise needs of your group with a couple of others. Draw up a graded series of questions, pitching them at a level which will encourage people to think hard without causing them to freeze with fear.

2 Write out the final list of questions and print copies if necessary.

3 Arrange a hall so that you can assemble the whole group together, but still break them up into threes when needed. The final debriefing might require a blackboard or overhead projector, and an expert panel.

4 Some participants may feel that they have performed very badly at the activity; others may wonder if they really do understand the Christian faith. Be ready to do some teaching at the close of the session, making sure your material is positive and encouraging. Prepare copies for participants.

5 If required, arrange for some assistants to help run the activity. It is wise to have one organiser for every 15 players. The key role of these organisers is to keep the small groups running smoothly by offering help and encouragement.

RUNNING THE ACTIVITY

This is how the activity might run with older teens:

3.00 Hold a final briefing with your assistants, and check that everything is ready to go.

3.15 Welcome the participants and explain the activity to them. Allow time for questions. Form the small groups, each of three people.

3.30 Run a suitable 'warm up' activity to relax everyone. It may be wise to do this in a way that involves the small groups as units. This will build trust in the 'threes' you have formed. For ideas on how to warm up, see page 47.

3.50 Ask players to form groups of three and to decide who will be the first observer, interviewer, and interviewee. Repeat the essential rules, reveal the first topic, and let the first role-play begin. When the set time (e.g. 3 minutes) has expired for the first role-play, sound a bell, and ask each group to spend

5 minutes reviewing what happened.
- 4.00 Call the session to order, and announce that the second role-play should begin. Reveal the second topic. People need to 'rotate' in the functions of observer, interviewer and interviewee, to give each a turn. This process continues until all the topics have been covered, or until one hour has passed. Remember that many participants will find this rather draining.
- 4.30 When the topics have all been tackled, or exhaustion has set in, call the group back together for a careful debriefing. See page 12 for ideas. Encourage all players to share their feelings, the lessons learnt and the questions they now have. If the group is very close knit, players may be able to discuss some of the difficulties they experienced. Wind up with some helpful teaching, some encouragement and worship.

ESSENTIAL RULES

1 Stay together in your group of three. You will be told when to start acting out each 3 minute interview and when time is up. You then have 5 minutes to talk about how it went. After that, the signal will go to begin a new interview.

2 You will do each interview topic once only. You will rotate in your roles as interviewer, interviewee, and observer. These roles are as follows.
- 'Interviewer' — ask the question provided. Be friendly, interested and encouraging. Keep asking for some information.
- 'Interviewee' — give your honest and personal answer to the question. Avoid jargon, be coherent, and be friendly.
- 'Observer' — watch out for jargon, incoherency, and interesting emotions. Point these out during the discussion time.

3 Save any controversies until the end of the activity when we will reassemble. You will be able to toss these at the panel of experts.

4 As you progress from one question to the next, you may find it increasingly difficult to share your thoughts. Please continue as long as possible before asking to be excused from the role of interviewee. You can still participate as interviewer or as observers. Remember that this exercise is designed to help you grow.

5 Because all participants will be sharing their personal feelings and beliefs, you need to treat answers as confidential. During discussion times you may politely disagree with the statement of another group member, but should avoid 'flying at their throat'. There will be time at the conclusion of the program to clarify matters of Christian belief.

SAMPLES

Questions

An instruction card worded as follows would suit Christians with little experience in verbalising their faith.

> *These are your questions, to be tackled in order:*
> - Who was Jesus Christ?
> - What did Jesus want to achieve?
> - Does the life of Jesus still matter today?
> - What are the essentials of the Christian faith?
> - What effect has Christianity had on your life?
> - Why are you still a Christian?

VARIATIONS

1 The sample questions (above) would suit a wide age range. The overall style is gentle and encouraging. You could easily add a lot more aggression and challenge to stir up a group of veteran evangelists; the simplest way would be to issue secret role cards at the start of each round. For example, the interviewer could be instructed to act in a sarcastic and hostile manner. See the following activity in this chapter (No. 3, 'The blockage') for ideas on setting up more demanding situations.

2 If you need an exercise to suit your 'Agnostics Anonymous' group, devise questions which assume no personal faith, but which help players to think through key issues. Questions might include-
- What evidence exists that Jesus was a historical person?
- If Jesus really existed, was he mad, bad, or divine?

3 Insist that players tackle every question provided.

2. The blockage

12 - 100 | 1.5 - 2 hours | 12 - 100

DESCRIPTION

This is a challenging training exercise for Christians who are often engaged in apologetics (the exciting art of showing that Christianity makes sense). The exercise assumes that the participants have a good grasp of the Christian faith and of other belief systems in their community. A small group acts out a dialogue between Christians and their opponents, while the audience studies every move. The role-play stops, and discussion follows. The role-plays equip players to be sensitive to the needs of others, and more confident in dealing with different styles of opposition. By acting in the roles of 'observer', 'Christian', and 'opponent', they gain a fuller understanding of apologetics. There are some traps in the exercise, which looks at a number of classic communication blockages. In places the script calls for the 'Christians' to make some serious mistakes; this should ensure a lively debriefing for all concerned.

CHECKLIST

- Role cards for each group and each leader (see Samples).
- Bible, paper and pen for each participant.
- Resource notes for each participant.

PREPARATION

1 Sample roles are provided. To prepare your own, first find out what your group's needs are. Do they often debate with intellectuals, with Muslims, with Marxists, or with lazy sun-loving pleasure seekers? Do they face apathy, missiles, or ridicule? What sort of help do they really need? You must get this part right or the role-plays chosen will not meet the needs of the participants.

2 Appoint some suitable leaders (one per 12 players) to help you run the activity and ask them to help you assemble a few realistic and challenging role-plays. Prepare copies for players and for the leaders in charge.

3 Ensure that participants will bring pens and paper to jot down observations while each scene is being acted out.

4 Arrange a hall so that a stage area is clearly visible and the acoustics allow all to hear. There must be space for groups to gather and prepare their items.

5 Some resources, positive teaching, and encouragement would be appropriate at the end. Have all this ready to go.

RUNNING THE ACTIVITY

The activity might run like this:

3.00 Welcome the participants and explain the program. Allow time for questions, and then run a suitable 'warm-up' activity. See page 47.

3.30 Divide participants into groups of 4-12 and give each group a different role-play. They will need time to prepare these, because some of the scenes are demanding. Leaders will need to move about, offering assistance and ensuring that quality is high. Check that all are ready before calling the groups to order. Remind everyone to face the audience while performing.

3.50 Call the first group to come forward. Remind the audience of the need to jot down significant points as they emerge during the role-play. Stop the performance when the points have been made, thank the group (applause may be in order) and keep them up front while their performance is analysed. Ask the audience to guess the performers' instructions and to comment on the general lessons learnt from the item, especially

concerning ways to deal with communication blockages.
4.00 Call the second group forward. Repeat the above pattern until all role-plays have been acted out.
4.35 Wind up the session with some helpful instruction, encouragement and resources. A strongly positive conclusion is vital, because some participants may feel very much aware of their weaknesses.
4.55 Thank all participants, and close with appropriate Bible readings (e.g. Colossians 4:5-6) and prayer.

SAMPLES

Roles for novices

These instructions could be used with younger teens or inexperienced adults. Scenes could be played with two, or as many as six people (e.g. three play the Christians, and three the friends).

1 'The gabbler'
Christian — Very keen to get a new friend to come along to a church youth event on a Saturday. Chatters away at high volume, telling of the great program, and ignores the friend's attempts to speak.
Friend — Very polite, and tries in vain to get a word in. Finally manages to explain that their family are devout Jews who worship on Saturdays.

2 'The yes butter'
Christian — Does everything right, showing warmth and patience in inviting the friend to a special church youth event. Handles the excuses and arguments of the friend well.
Friend — Admits that the event sounds attractive, but comes up with loads of silly excuses (e.g. 'A Mormon on a bicycle ran over the family cat', 'I might not find the church hall', 'I hate pipe organs').

3 'Daniel meets Dr Lion'
Christian — Very friendly and talkative, steering the conversation towards religious beliefs. Tries hard to answer the friend's questions, but finds some too deep and offers to return with answers after doing some research.
Friend — Serious and thoughtful, asking plenty of questions (e.g. 'Who made God?', 'Who wrote the Bible?', 'How could God die on the cross?').

4 'The pie-high believer'
Christian — Brushes aside a number of thoughtful questions from the friend, and chatters about the emotional 'high' offered by worship at their church. Feelings, and not facts are what matters.
Friend — Keeps asking serious, and very basic, questions about reading the Bible, being saved, going to Heaven, etc. Gradually reveals that Mum is dying of cancer and also wants some answers.

5 'What colour is red?'
Christian — Wants to avoid being known as a Christian, and tries everything to change the topic to sport or gossip. Appears to be ashamed of faith, despite being a member of a healthy church.
Friend — Hungry for information about the Christian's church involvement. Asks lots of basic questions about what Christians believe and what happens at youth group. Keeps ignoring the red herrings, and steers the conversation back to religious belief.

Roles for advanced players

These instructions were used with some talented older teens, and would best suit a group of 2-6 players (e.g. Three play the Christians, three play the rest).

1 'Listening to the needs'
Christian — Keen to score a conversion, and interested only in the friend's 'spiritual' needs. Ignores all clues that friend may want to talk about some deep personal needs.
Friend — Polite and quiet. Agnostic beliefs, but shows little interest in argument. Keeps trying to hint at major personal problems (parent with cancer, engagement about to break up, etc).

2 'Pardon my cliche'
Christian — Keen, aggressive, insensitive. Knows all the right Bible verses, and can smell an easy victory here. Explains friend's resistance in condescending terms ('... you must be under conviction of sin'), using every bit of jargon in the book.
Friend — Starts off showing mild interest in the gospel, but becomes more confused and irritated as the cliches heap up. Finally declares the conversation a waste of time, and storms off.

ROLE PLAYS

3 'To catch a red herring'
Christian — Invites friend to a local church meeting. The friend refuses, and attacks the Church. Christian gives a good defence but puts most energy into relating the gospel to the friend's real needs.
Friend — Reacts vigorously to the invitation by ridiculing the worldwide Church. Has some vulnerable points (e.g. no purpose in life, lots of guilt, but tries to evade personal questions by using red herrings.

4 'A little knowledge is a dangerous thing'
Christian — Patiently tries to untangle the friend's jumbled thinking. Puts a lot of effort into asking clarifying questions and setting out the distinctives of Christianity.
Friend — Claims to have a good grasp of religious matters, but has no real knowledge of any one faith. Easily drifts from Islam to Bahai to Zen, asserting confidently that they are all the same.

5 'How to please a pushy pagan'
Christian — Quiet and confident, tries to give good clear answers and to relate things to their personal experience. Very patient and friendly.
Friend — Aggressive and confrontational. Loudly claims that the Bible was faked, that the Church causes suffering and that prayer is laughable. Makes no attempt to listen, but tries to humiliate and embarrass the Christian.

6 'Tried it, and nothing happened'
Christian — Well-meaning and friendly, but is too quick to brush aside the other person's doubts. No empathy or sensitivity at all. Initially insists that friend is still saved, but concludes by demanding repentance and conversion.
Friend — Fragile, quiet, sensitive, and rather cynical, because of a failed attempt to become a Christian. Still sympathetic, but no faith.

7 'Anything to please'
Christian — Tries to prove that friend can have all his politics and be a Christian. Keen on liberation theology, but has lost the distinctives of Christianity.
Friend — Committed Marxist, convinced of the reality of class war. Attracted to 'Jesus the Liberator', and open to know more about the Jesus of the New Testament. Has zero interest in the supernatural, however, and denies that sin exists.

VARIATIONS

1 If you have an articulate, fast-thinking group, add excitement by asking the opposing sides of each role-play to prepare secretly. This way, the 'Christians' have no idea what sort of arguments they will face. Both sides still receive the same general instructions, but neither knows exactly what they will have to deal with.

2 By adjusting the level of the role-plays, this activity can be used with kids as young as ten to twelve. Quite raw new Christians can also benefit from it. It is simply a matter of knowing your group's needs and their level of spiritual maturity.

3. Conflict at home

DESCRIPTION

This activity can have quite an impact on both parents and children, largely because of its potential for role-reversal work. Teenagers acting out the role of a conscientious parent will suddenly realise what it must be like for their own parents. The same goes for parents who act out the role of a 'repressed' teenager. Participants act out a number of conflicts and try to win at all costs. After a thoughtful debriefing and Bible study, the same role-plays are repeated, but this time all the players work hard to arrive at a happy compromise.

CHECKLIST

- Role cards for players, in envelopes (see Samples)
- Resource materials on relationships, and Bibles for all participants.

PREPARATION

1 You should do this role-play with people whom you know fairly well. This is because you need to match people carefully to the different roles. You could give a headstrong youth the role of a 'very worried parent' and pit him against a 'reckless 13-year-old girl who wants to stay out until 1.00 am'. In undertaking such deliberate role-reversals, use a little disguise (as in the previous sentence), otherwise your players may mutiny on you. Don't make more than 25 per cent of the scenes into deliberate role-reversals. Samples are provided (for use with secondary school students). If you are creating your own role-plays, ensure that they cover a wide range of situations, and ask a friend to check them for you.

2 Write these out on cards for all the players, keeping copies for yourself and any assistants. Prepare some suitable material on family relationships, and ensure that Bibles will be available. You might also want to arrange supplies of relevant books for sale.

3 Arrange a hall so that there is a suitable area for the actors and seating for the preparation and performance phases.

RUNNING THE ACTIVITY

With a group of parents, the activity might run like this:

- 7.00 Prepare the hall with seating, lights, supper, bookstall, soft music.
- 7.15 Welcome parents as they arrive. Introduce them to the leaders of the youth group. Issue name tags if needed.
- 7.20 Explain the evening program. Answer any questions. Run a thorough warm-up session (see page 47). Remember that adults are often very inhibited and nervous about getting involved in this sort of thing. Issue role cards in named envelopes, and allow time for groups to form and plan.
- 7.45 Begin the first round of role-plays, being sure to involve yourself in one of the early ones. Invite brief responses at the end of each little confrontation.
- 8.00 Hold a major debriefing of the action so far. Encourage some honest sharing of the pressures felt by parents of teenage children. Provide some confidence-building input (e.g. by video or guest speaker) and explore the Bible together (e.g. noting the double edge of Ephesians 6:1-4).
- 8.30 Allow a few minutes for groups to re-form and to plan their second run. This time they are to seek happy resolution, not confrontation.

ROLE PLAYS

Encourage some brief comments at the end of each performance as well as applause and personal thanks.

8.50 Wind up the evening. Invite parents to inspect the bookstall, and to stay for supper. Close off with a short time of worship.

SAMPLES

Role plays

The following samples have worked well with students of secondary-school age. Each role play needs one or two 'parents' and one or two 'kids'. Note that the roles lack precise detail, which means that they can be used with kids from any social level. Feel free to add local colour with references to local industries, school and so on. Remember to tell players whether you want a 'confrontation' or a 'peaceful resolution' to the problem.

---

1 'Leaving school'

The hard-working parents have had little formal education, and have struggled all their lives to get where they are. They are paying off a modest home, and have secure jobs which they don't particularly enjoy. They don't want their kids to repeat their mistakes. Predictably, they want their children to gain a good education. The children are legally old enough to leave school, and have just announced their intention to do exactly that. They are optimistic that they can find some sort of work, and that this will be better than more school uniforms and exams.

---

2 'The smokers'

Parents
— you both smoke heavily, and have done so for the last 30 years. Although Uncle Fred died of lung cancer last year (aged 47), you have no intention of giving up smoking, as you have few pleasures. You have been conscientious in your care for your children, providing them with good schooling and a comfortable home.

Children
— you intensely dislike the stale smell of tobacco around the house, and worry about your parents' health. You want them to overcome their addiction, because of the expense and the medical arguments about the perils of 'active' and 'passive' smoking. You enjoy excellent health, and your sporting achievements are considerable.

---

3 'The big party'

The whole family is invited to a large and lavish 21st birthday party. The proud hosts are wealthy, status conscious, and distantly related. You know that the guest list includes your richest relatives, father's business partners, local V.I.P.s, and a number of your close personal friends.

Parents
— you wish to go, and insist that your children dress in the most elegant formal wear (e.g. tuxedo, ball gown, hair professionally done).

Children
— you are reluctant to attend such a 'stuffy' event. You refuse to be humiliated in front of your school mates by being seen in such formal regalia. You fear that the other teens present will be dressed in designer casual clothing.

---

4 'Saturday morning'

Mum and Dad work long hours from Monday to Friday, and expect their children to help them with all the chores on Saturday mornings. There is usually a whole week's supply of washing, cleaning, gardening, and shopping to do. Once this is done, everyone is free to enjoy the rest of the weekend. The kids are competent athletes, and have just been invited to join 'A' grade teams. This level of competition is always held on Saturday mornings, and the kids would return home exhausted around 1.00 pm.

---

5 'The youth group'

Parents
— you are members of a small conservative church. The pastor is a close family friend, and means well. You concede that the church has almost no young people, probably because it is so old fashioned. You have many relatives and old friends there.

Children
— you bear no grudges, but feel the need to leave your present church and join a flourishing new one (of the same denomination). This features three youth pastors and a huge youth program, plus a large percentage of your friends in its congregation.

6 'Freedom to choose'

Parents

— you are very narrow-minded and insist that God does not exist. You will not allow a Bible into the house, and destroy any religious material in the junk mail in case your children are contaminated. You regularly write to the principal of your children's school to protest about the existence of religious education and of a Christian student group there. You firmly believe in freedom from Christian 'propaganda'.

Children

— many of your school-friends attend a lunchtime group where the Christian faith is discussed. They have invited you to attend the local church youth-group on Friday evenings. A highly respected teacher from your school helps run it. You are keen to attend, because the social program is great, and the discussion times give you freedom to make up your own mind about the Christian faith.

7 'The video night'

Parents

— you consider yourselves to be fairly broad-minded, and have provided your kids with ample information concerning human sexuality. You believe that Christian sexual standards make sense, and have communicated this to your children. You have carefully controlled the types of television programs they watch as well as monitoring the magazines they read. You have so far had no grounds for concern regarding their behaviour.

Children

— you have generally gone along quite happily with your parents' moral outlook, but do want some freedom to choose your own values. You have just arrived home with some friends to watch a video you have hired. Titled *The Last Days of Sodom and Gomorrah*, it won 12 Academy Awards and is based on the book by an eminent English author. You are greatly embarrassed when your parents order you not to show it.

VARIATIONS

1 This activity could be adapted to meet the needs of all adult groups who have responsibility for the care of young people. Conflict at home concerns teachers, youth workers, counsellors and pastors. The age-range of the children involved could also be quite broad, extending to older primary students. Teenagers who are out in the work force can also benefit.

2 For a really interesting evening, why not call parents and children together for a joint program? Tact and care would be needed, but a lot of excitement and learning could result. Imagine the sight of a parent asking permission to go to a party, and two 12-year-olds pouring out an avalanche of parental doubts and fears.

4. Don't apologise

12 - 100   1.5 - 2 hours   10 - 100

DESCRIPTION

This exercise is designed to help players cope with pressure from aggressive non-Christians. They are given problem situations where Christians find themselves on the receiving end of some hostile or teasing remarks. They think through the problem, come up with some creative solutions, then write a role-play script which incorporates these solutions and perform it. The context can be the school, home, or workplace environment of young (or older) Christians. Players are encouraged not to apologise when challenged about their faith, but to respond with directness, love and humour.

CHECKLIST

- A problem card for each group of players (see Samples)
- A Bible and some resource material for each participant (see Sample Bible references)

PREPARATION

1 Sample role plays (for use with young teenagers) have been provided. If you need to prepare your own, you must know the everyday situation of the players very intimately. Talk with them to find out what sort of treatment they get from their non-Christian acquaintances and how adequate their response to this treatment is. Having done your research, write a batch of problem situations, and ask others to check them.

2 Print the best of these, producing copies for players, yourself, and any helpers.

3 Some players may lack the ability to create suitable solutions to your problems. Help them to invent their 'own' solution by providing biblical teaching, case studies, videos, and lists of basic principles. You may need to tackle a few examples together before splitting up into small groups, or you could simply provide 'optional resources'. You should have some assistants who will be ready to help groups if needed.

4 Prepare a hall so that there is space for the final presentations and for the small-group preparation.

5 Have some resource material ready for the conclusion of the session. This should be strongly encouraging, because it is possible that some players will feel most inadequate by the end of the evening.

RUNNING THE ACTIVITY

The activity might run like this:

7.00 Welcome the participants and explain what is going to happen. Answer any questions.

7.20 Run a warm-up session (see page 47) and form small groups.

7.35 Allow the members of each small group to share some of their personal stories of being heckled by their non-Christian friends.

7.45 Hand out the role-cards and give groups time to think out their answers. Some players are sure to need resources and assistance. If appropriate, demonstrate to the whole group how the problems could be handled.

8.10 Ask each group in turn to read out their card and to perform the role-play. As each finishes, applaud, then invite questions and some constructive criticism.

8.40 Wind up the evening with some encouragement and Bible teaching. Beware of demoralising some players, who will be feeling inadequate. If appropriate, conclude with a time of prayer in the small groups, with members sharing their needs and problems.

SAMPLES

Bible passages

The following passages show Jesus and his followers under verbal attack. Acts 17:16-34 (Paul in Athens), John 4:5-30 (Jesus and the woman at the well), Matthew 11:16-30 and 23:24 (pungent humour from Jesus), Acts 2:13-16 (Peter replies to hecklers).

Look for evidence of the following in their replies:
- a willingness to find common ground, if it exists.
- a touch of humour, to lighten the situation.
- genuine love for the other person.
- directness and honesty.

Role-plays
The following role-plays were drawn up for young teenagers.

1
An intelligent friend insists loudly that 'God is dead', and tries hard to convince you. The people you usually have lunch with are all listening. How do you respond?

2
You are new at school, and have just been accepted by the 'in' group in your form. On Monday, during recess, the talk turns to what happened over the weekend. Most of your friends, it seems, indulged in wild parties, romantic flings, and a bit of shoplifting, while you spent the weekend practising musical items for the youth service at church. To your horror, you realise that all eyes are on you. What do you say?

3
A few Christian kids at your school have set up a lunchtime group. None of your friends are remotely interested, but you have promised to attend this lunchtime. Just as you get up to go there, one of your friends comments 'Don't tell me, you're going off to sing hymns I suppose!' How do you respond?

4
You are sitting in the back seat of the bus with your friends when one of them starts to tell a joke that 'would make a prostitute blush'. As the joke grows fouler, you realise that some in the group are watching to see how you will respond. One of them remarks that you are too much of a saint to even enjoy a good joke. What could you do?

5
You have decided that drinking alcohol is a 'bad witness', partly because so many of your classmates get blind drunk on weekends. Now you are at a wedding, and all the glasses have been filled with champagne for the toasts. Someone whispers loudly in your ear that you will have to 'lower your standards', or else insult the happy couple. How would you reply?

6
The basketball team are all getting changed after practice, and the talk turns to sexual conquests. One by one, all of your team mates claim to have been sexually active over the last year. Your neighbour turns to you with a nasty leer saying 'Don't tell me you're still a virgin! What's the matter with you?' How should you respond?

5. Church at war

DESCRIPTION

This activity is an introduction to the noble art of peace-making via a taste of some bitter disputes inside the Church. The action begins with some fiery confrontations in which neither side wants to give any ground. After some discussion and teaching, the scenes are repeated, with participants now working hard to create peace. Precise instructions mean that a wide range of personality types and peacemaking styles are seen in action. Players explore the biblical perspectives on peace, and discover how to put this knowledge into practice.

CHECKLIST

- Role cards for groups and for leaders (see Samples)
- A Bible for each participant (see Sample Bible references)

PREPARATION

1 Sample role plays (suitable for young adults) have been provided. If you need to prepare your own, think carefully about the types of conflicts which the participants have to cope with. Design role plays which will be reasonably true to life, and which will give breadth to the exercise. If it starts to look too heavy, throw in a couple of wickedly exaggerated scenes.

2 Ask some friends to check the role-plays for any faults, and then print role-cards for players, yourself, and any helpers.

3 Some positive teaching will be needed at the midway point of the session, so prepare your resources in advance. Find out what the Hebrew word for peace ('shalom') really means. Use Bible passages, books on interpersonal effectiveness, case studies and short stories. Unless this is well packaged, players may not be able to complete the second half of the exercise.

4 Prepare a hall so that there is space for explanation, preparation, and for the acting out of the various scenes.

5 Prepare an encouraging conclusion to the evening which revises the main points.

RUNNING THE ACTIVITY

The activity might run like this:
1.00 Hold a final briefing with your fellow leaders.
1.30 Welcome the participants and explain the activity. Run a suitable 'warm-up' exercise (see page 47). Form small groups.
1.50 Hand out the role cards and allow preparation time. Check that all groups are able to cope with their tasks.
2.00 Ask each group in turn to come out and present their scene of confrontation. Allow for some audience response in each case, to drive home the pain and seriousness of the situation.
2.30 Provide some positive teaching on conflict resolution, using the Bible and any other resources that help players to understand the dynamics of making peace. (See Samples and Variations.) Instruct players to re-enact their scenes so that peace and justice prevail. Some groups may need help.
3.10 Each group performs again, and the audience provides constructive criticism.
3.30 When all have acted out their scenes, provide a helpful and encouraging conclusion. Some gentle singing and worship might be a good way to wind down.

SAMPLES

Role plays

These were used for young adults, all mature Christians.

1

The youth group members have spent months organising a big fund-raising ball, the profits from which should be enough to pay off the debt on the War Memorial chapel. The advertising and tickets for the ball have gone out. The elders are furious that the church hall is to be 'contaminated' with loud rock music and alcohol, as they had presumed that the function would be more restrained. With only 2 weeks to go, the elders confront the youth group leaders. (Form two teams of elders and youth leaders. Together, plan a blazing, fruitless shouting match.)

2

The new church vestry is having its first meeting. A number of the 'old guard' have been replaced by young professionals. When the treasurer reads out the financial summaries, a discussion concerning Communion Bread suddenly erupts. The new members move a motion that 'No more special Communion Wafers be purchased, and that stone-ground, Pritikin-approved, wholemeal rolls be used instead'. The elderly parish priest is horrified, as are the senior vestry members, all aged 60-70. (Take on the roles of Priest, Old Vestry, and Young Vestry. Plan a fiery, emotional confrontation.)

3

The new outer-suburban church is bursting at the seams. The youth group has doubled over the last year, and is set to pass 150 members by Christmas. As the Sunday service ends, the pastor invites some of the youth leaders (all volunteers) to make an announcement. The congregation is stunned to hear that this excellent leadership team is unable to cope with their responsibilities, and is demanding that a full-time youth pastor be hired. As debate continues, it becomes obvious that the salary for a youth pastor would come at the expense of the large overseas missions budget. (Enact the closing minutes of this heated debate, representing the missions group and voluntary leaders with equal vigour and determination.)

4

The new vicar, the choirmaster and the chairman of Parish Council get along famously. They are all steeped in the ancient traditions of the Church and long to stem the modernist tide. Sorting out the choir is one of their priorities. At the weekly choir practice, the ladies are stunned to get a posy of flowers each, and a letter thanking them for their years of service. They have been sacked to make way for a male choir which is in the finest English ecclesiastical tradition. (Plan a savage verbal brawl between the female choristers and the advocates of male vocal supremacy.)

5

The small rural church has made do with modest buildings for a long time. A wave of upwardly-mobile new members complain that these facilities are drab and lack comfort. A special general meeting has been called, and a motion put 'That a $1,500,000 appeal be launched to build a new hall and church.' The movers of the motion have spoken boldly of massive growth, increased giving and positive thinking. Strong opposition comes from lower-income members of the church, who would rather spend money on people ministry than on 'bricks and mortar'. (Act out the savage closing round of the general meeting, where Young's Analytical Concordances fly with deadly aim. Provide a weak chairperson, some new members, and some low income members.)

6

Your huge old inner-suburban church is to be classified by the National Trust, and features superb stained glass, antique furnishings and a congregation of 32. Some bureaucrats from denominational head quarters come to visit and insist on some massive changes. In return for financial assistance (about 50 per cent of total running costs), the church must 'market' its facilities. For example, they propose hiring out the main worship area to orchestras, recording companies, and theatre groups. (Continue this discussion, making it as emotional as possible. Some of you are the bureaucrats, and the rest are horrified locals.)

ROLE PLAYS

Bible readings
- 2 Kings 6:8-23 — enemies are killed with kindness.
- 1 Kings 3:16-28 — justice leaves a winner and a loser.
- 1 Corinthians 12 — respect diversity inside unity.
- Acts 15:1-35 — peaceful compromise is reached.
- Ephesians 4:26-27 — resolve conflicts promptly.
- Galatians 5:13-15 — respect your opponent's needs.

VARIATIONS

1 The samples provided relate to the title of this exercise, 'Church at War'. You may need to change the setting to a school, youth group, home, or workplace, however the dynamics of 'waging peace' do not vary all that much.

2 If your players need something a little more stretching, why not issue secret instructions concerning the second wave of performances. You could ask some groups to seek peace at any price, and others to refuse a peaceful settlement no matter how generous the offers. This should generate some vigorous debate at the end of each performance.

3 Many Church disputes involve matters of unity and of truth. 'Unity' relates to quality of relationships, and 'truth' describes one's loyalty to principles. These two qualities can be marked on the arms of a graph, with which you chart the progress of each side in a role play. This shows for example, whether unity is sacrificed in the quest for truth. A perfect solution would mean both sides agree that truth has not been compromised, and that unity is fully restored.

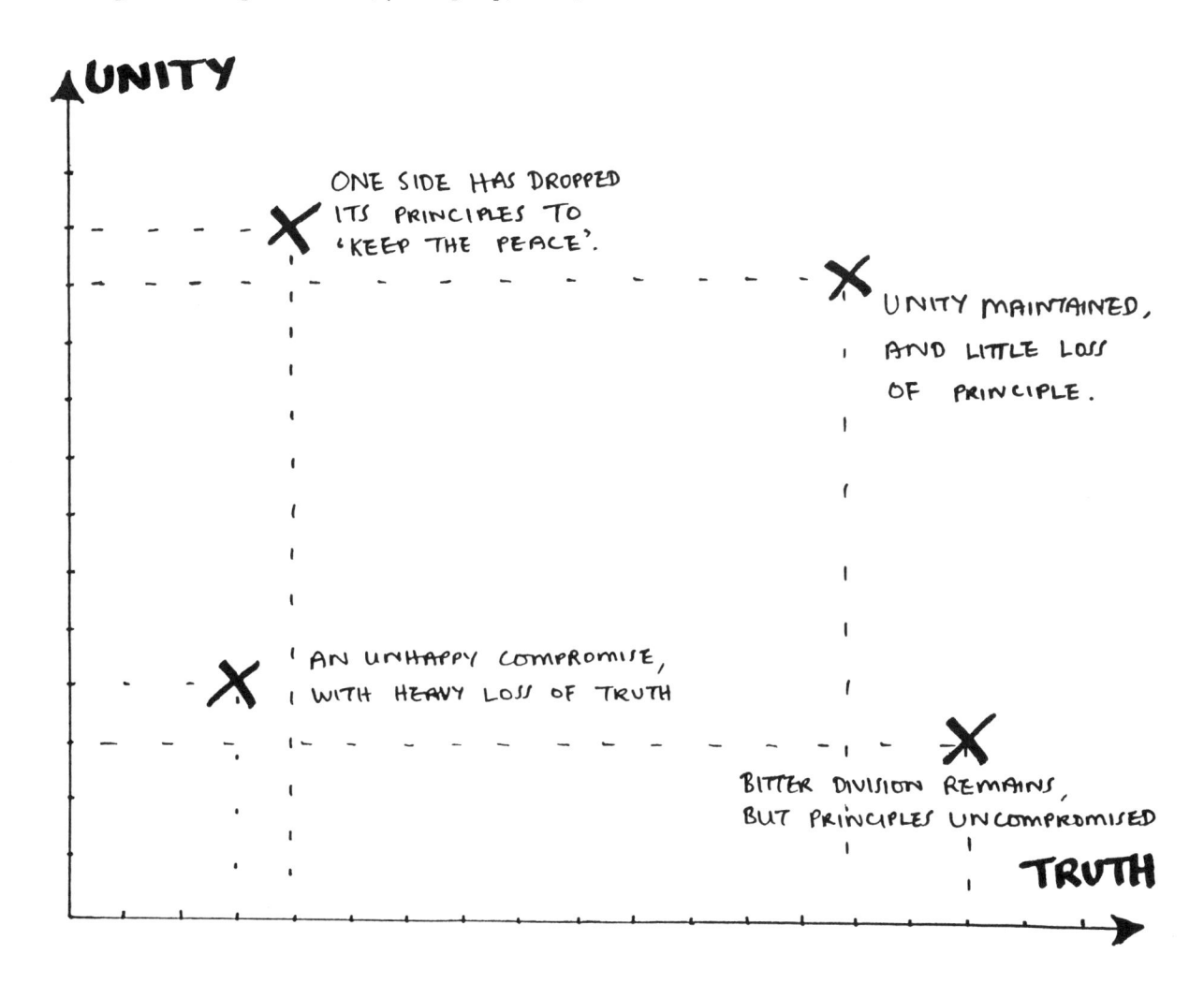

Graph with axes UNITY (vertical) and TRUTH (horizontal), showing four marked points:
- *Upper left:* ONE SIDE HAS DROPPED ITS PRINCIPLES TO 'KEEP THE PEACE'.
- *Upper right:* UNITY MAINTAINED, AND LITTLE LOSS OF PRINCIPLE.
- *Lower left:* AN UNHAPPY COMPROMISE, WITH HEAVY LOSS OF TRUTH
- *Lower right:* BITTER DIVISION REMAINS, BUT PRINCIPLES UNCOMPROMISED

Chapter four
Enacted Bible readings

What are enacted Bible readings?

For starters, they are Bible readings. Some use the text of the Bible as it is, while some modify it to communicate more effectively. Either way, the intention is to bring the passage to life for a modern audience while staying faithful to the original teaching point. The 'enacted' bit is important. As the passage is read aloud, some (or all) of those present mime the various scenes. For example, in some churches the whole congregation has spontaneously recreated the 'Palm Sunday' procession of Jesus into Jerusalem. Other churches have arranged for a small team to rehearse a script until they can mime it at professional standard. In either case, there is no need to learn a script; all the cues come from the story. The actors are simply given their identity (or 'role') and then immerse themselves in the events as the narrator relates them. No prior acting experience is necessary.

Why use them?

Some passages from the Bible tell the story so clearly that modern hearers understand at once. No modification may be needed. In many cases, however, the passage is so familiar, so brief, or so culturally obscure that the original teaching point is lost to modern audiences. Some careful script-writing can recapture the original shock value, humour, or suspense of an ancient story. The examples set out later in this chapter have motivated many people, of all ages, to get their Bibles off the shelf and to start reading them. That should be a key aim of any enacted reading. Enacted Bible readings are a useful tool for Christian ministry because they combine the best features of story-telling and role-playing. The story element not only captures people's interest, arouses their imagination and sends them on a journey into a different world, it also drives home the teaching points in a very memorable way. People's minds and bodies are immersed in the scene, enabling total involvement, which is a wonderful aid to understanding and remembering.

How do I make sure it works?

It is wise to start small before running any event with a sizeable cast. As you learn how to write and read scripts for small groups, you will gain the skills and confidence to work successfully with different age-groups and larger numbers. Experience also enables you to be a more relaxed 'producer', spontaneously helping your audience to become fully involved in the story. Of course, no enacted reading will survive bad preparation, distracting mannerisms, monotone voices, or confused aims. In many ways, however, the following activities are the most 'idiot-proof' ones in this book.

How do I know if it worked?

No activity in this book has 'worked' unless lives are changed in some way — and of course, it takes time to see results of that kind. However a simple test of the effectiveness of an enacted reading is to ask the participants to tell the story back to you in their own words. If they reveal that they have grasped the central teaching points, then you have obviously done a good job.

How do I write my own?

Whether you are adapting one of the examples in

ENACTED BIBLE READINGS

this chapter, or starting from zero, there are some essentials in every good enacted reading. They can be summarised thus:

1 Aim to drive home clearly one big teaching point in the story. You should be able to express this point in a single sentence. (There may of course be some minor lessons on the way, too.)

2 A concise summary at the end of the story is valid, but avoid giving a tail-end 'sermon'. The best place to emphasise a teaching point is at the most exciting parts of the story. Learn the art of weaving it into the flow of events (e.g. 'For a moment David wondered if God was really behind this mad adventure. Then, even as he hesitated, he remembered the time he fought the giant.'). Refine a script until it is perfect.

3 Anticipate questions about culture and theology, and weave the answers into the fabric of the story. Graphic language will handle most problems, but the odd visual aid is quite legitimate if shown briefly.

4 To fire the audience's imagination, use language that appeals to the senses. Describe smells, sounds, textures, and tastes. Choose verbs that are truly expressive (e.g. replace 'ate' with 'wolfed down').

5 Know the story so well that you can spontaneously adjust it. Tell it with your hands, body, eyes and tone of voice and as you do so, let your gaze sweep over the audience, so that each person feels that the story is for them alone.

6 Use as much direct speech as possible (e.g. 'Go home!', she roared).

7 Don't hesitate to embellish a biblical passage if the end result better expresses the original drama, humour or teaching point. The most common way of doing this is to add colourful (and plausible) details to the story (e.g. add the jokes lobbed at Noah as he built the Ark).

8 If the audience knows the story too well, set the scene in the present day, or deliberately add a shock ending (e.g. the Good Samaritan taunts the injured Jew, and then bludgeons him to death).

9 If the actors do not read the script in advance, you must build very clear hints into it. Give clear warning if major manoeuvres are called for (e.g. 'they prepared to fire the arrows'). You, or an assistant, may need to help actors mime their way through some scenes. For example, show them how to hold their imaginary bows and arrows or how to peer out from an imaginary window.

Where do I start?

The following examples have been used with excellent results. Read through them and you will soon see how they work. Then go and try some out with a co-operative small group.

1. The pearl

DESCRIPTION

This reading dramatises the very short parable about the trader who sells all to buy the perfect pearl (Matthew 13:45-46). There is a touch of comedy to capture the interest of older players, and snippets of cultural information are added, but the emphasis is on the dramatic price paid for the pearl. No rehearsal is needed, but it is best to give players clear roles, and to show them how they could act out their scenes. After a brief and enjoyable production, the scene is set for a discussion. Adults often flounder as they attempt to pin down the full meaning of the parable, yet children are enabled to grasp its essential message. Typically, a new interest in the parables is born.

CHECKLIST

- A script for the narrator (see Samples)
- A Bible for each participant
- Copies of discussion questions for leaders (see Samples)
- Props and costumes (if desired)

PREPARATION

1 Find out the needs of your group. This mainly affects the final discussion process, but may require some shift of emphasis in the script itself.

2 Before writing your script, read the passage in the translation normally used by the audience. Ensure that the script explains any difficult words or ideas presented in that translation.

3 Prepare discussion questions at a suitable level, and ensure that all group members will have access to a Bible. Ask a friend to check both script and questions. Copy questions for group leaders.

4 Make sure that the 'stage' area is adequate for size and visibility, and that the narrator will be clearly heard.

5 Meet with any co-leaders to discuss both script and questions. Issue copies of questions.

RUNNING THE ACTIVITY

This is how the activity might run:

1.00 Meet with any co-leaders and check that preparations are complete.

1.15 Explain the activity to the group, and answer any questions. Stress the need for them to let their imagination flow, and to get fully involved with their roles. If the group needs to be warmed-up before they will act, see page 47.

1.30 Involving your co-leaders, assign roles and give some tips on how to act out each scene. See the casting instructions on page 65. A creative group may not need any assistance.

1.40 The show begins. Read the script aloud, watching closely for signs that the players need clearer direction. Ensure that the 'end product' is good enough to drive home the teaching point. If not, repeat the show.

1.50 Form small discussion groups and distribute Bibles. Participants then find the original passage, read it and wrestle with the questions (See Samples). If appropriate, call everybody back together and ask groups to report on their findings.

2.10 Close with a time of reflection and prayer, centred on the main teaching point of the passage.

SAMPLES

Casting instructions

ENACTED BIBLE READINGS

Select and prepare the cast as follows:
- Pearl trader — imposing, fat, waddling, slow; sunglasses, Arab costume.
- Other trader — as above, but less spectacular.
- Grovelling slave — holds imaginary tray, permanently cringes very low.
- Flock of fat sheep — the more the merrier, on all fours, bleating.
- Herd of fast camels — lots of them, haughty, spitting action, nose up.
- Harem of beautiful women — wriggling sensuously.
- Pearl-market furniture — people become furniture, e.g. chairs and table.
  (Remind 'furniture' and slave to leap into action as soon as the word 'market' is mentioned in the script. Sheep, camels, and harem are to parade once across the stage whenever they are mentioned by the narrator.)

Script

(The script features italics for those words which are cues for the cast.)

Once, in a faraway land, lived a great pearl trader of enormous wealth and weight. He had everything he wanted, and loved to stand by his palace fountain each evening, counting his flock of *fat sheep* as they passed by, inspecting the teeth of his herd of *fast camels*, and winking at his harem of *beautiful women*. Each morning he would wake up, stretch, yawn, and waddle majestically down to the *pearl market*. There he would sit down and work hard all day at the thing he loved most, which was trading for pearls. He would greet another merchant, and drink polite cups of coffee which were constantly topped up by a grovelling slave. Then they would display to each other the very best pearls that they possessed. At the end of the day he would stand, stretch, yawn, and waddle majestically home. At dusk he would stand by the palace fountain and wink at his flock of *beautiful sheep*, count his herd of *fat camels*, and inspect the teeth of his *fast harem*. One morning he woke up, stretched, yawned, and waddled majestically down to the *pearl market*. He sat at his usual seat, greeted another merchant, and drank polite cups of coffee which were constantly topped up by a grovelling slave. Then they displayed to each other the very best pearls that they possessed.

And then he saw it. He saw it for the very first time! His eyes nearly popped out of his sunglasses. There before him, held by the other trader, was it, numero uno, the big one...It was a pearl of perfect colour, of immense size, of faultless quality and (quite predictably) of great price. He admired it, he touched it, he held it up to the light, he sniffed it, he licked it, and he liked it. In fact he loved it! It was perfect. He handed it back, asked what the price was, and fainted.

When he recovered, he stood, stretched, yawned, and hurried majestically home, deep in thought. He thought about the perfect pearl, and he thought about the price, which was equal to the value of all that he owned. He knew that this opportunity might never come again. Ever since he was thin he had yearned for the big one, the perfect pearl. He spent the whole night pacing to and fro in his room, and when he realised that the sun had risen, made his decision. For the last time, he stood by the palace fountain and inspected the teeth of his flock of *fast sheep*, winked at his herd of *beautiful camels*, and counted his *fat harem*. Then, driving them all before him, he jogged majestically down to the *pearl market*. He staggered to his usual seat, beckoned the other merchant, and gulped down a polite cup of coffee which was immediately refilled by the usual grovelling slave. He signed away all his worldly goods to the other merchant. He then solemnly received the perfect pearl in exchange. He stood, left the market, and was last seen walking off into the sunset, a very, very happy man.

Discussion questions

These would suit adults and older teens.
- What did Jesus mean by 'The Kingdom of Heaven'?
- Did the early Christians sell everything to gain the Kingdom?
- How did the discovery that the Son had risen affect the disciples?
- Do Christians today give up all they have to be saved?
- If religious persecution was to break out tomorrow, what sort of pressure would be enough to crush your church?
- What price would you put on your own faith, if pressured to drop it?

VARIATIONS

1 This script can be performed by a skilled mime troupe, or acted out spontaneously with a typical church congregation.

2 The teaching point will not be obscured if the whole script is updated to the present. Simply substitute 'arrogant chauffeurs' and 'limousines' for the camels, and so on.

3 It works well with a narrator reading and actors miming, but lines could be 'fed' to the cast. For example, if the narrator says that the merchant refused a coffee, the actor simply improvises, saying 'I won't have another coffee thanks.' Some narrators prefer to feed the exact words to the actor, who simply repeats them. Thus the narrator says, 'The merchant dazedly muttered "No more coffee thanks", and staggered off'. The actor repeats the words 'No more coffee thanks' then exits as directed.

2. David and Bathsheba

12 - 100   1 - 2 hours   10 - 100

DESCRIPTION

This reading follows King David through the sordid 'Bathsheba Affair' to the brave confrontation by Nathan, and to the desperate cry for forgiveness of Psalm 51. The narrative is based on II Samuel 11 and 12. There is a touch of comedy to hold the interest of those who are overfamiliar with the story, but overall, the mood is tragic, and there is scope for a group of serious actors to create considerable atmosphere. Although, like most enacted readings, it need not be rehearsed at all, some careful preparation by the main actors will give it a professional touch. As the reading draws to a solemn end, the scene is set for a discussion and some Bible reading. The teaching points are numerous, but 'biblical sexuality' and 'forgiveness' are obvious ones to consider. I have seen this enacted reading hold rough teenagers spellbound. It can also help jaded adults to rediscover the honesty and power of Scripture.

CHECKLIST

- A script for the narrator (see Samples)
- A Bible for each participant
- A copy of the discussion questions for each leader (see Samples)
- Costumes and props (if desired)

PREPARATION

1 A sample script and questions are provided, but you may need to adapt them to explore a relevant area more thoroughly. Find out the needs of your group.

2 To write your own script, read through the passage in the translation that the audience normally uses. Ensure that the script explains any difficult ideas or words presented in that translation.

3 Prepare discussion questions at a suitable level (see Samples) and ensure that all present will have access to a Bible. Show any co-leaders the script and questions, and check for any flaws.

4 Check that the hall to be used has a suitable stage area, and that the narrator will be clearly heard.

5 The narrator must know the script thoroughly, especially if a large audience is involved.

RUNNING THE ACTIVITY

This is how the activity might run:

1.00 Meet with co-leaders to ensure that preparations are complete.

1.15 Explain the activity to the group who will be doing the acting. This may well be the entire audience if crowd scenes are to be included. Stress the need for them to let their imagination flow, and to get fully involved in their roles. If the group needs to be 'warmed up' see page 47.

1.30 Assisted by your co-leaders, assign roles and give some tips on how to act out each scene. See the sample script below. A talented group may not need any preparation or assistance and may prefer to simply respond to the script.

1.40 The show begins, with the narrator watching for clues that the cast need clearer directions, or more time to respond to key lines. Rather than lose clarity of meaning, stop the show and repeat a section if necessary.

2.00 Form small discussion groups and allow the audience to talk about the performance and their personal response to it. Everyone should then read through the original biblical passages before tackling the discussion

ENACTED BIBLE READINGS

questions. Then, call everybody back together and ask groups to report on their findings.

2.10 Close with music and prayer, keeping minds focused on the main teaching point of the exercise.

SAMPLES

Cast

- King David — aloof expression, dignified movements, excited at times.
- Bathsheba — sensuous, sultry, proud, dignified.
- Sergeant Uriah — wholesome, crisp military movements, neat.
- Royal household — all very formal, lots of bowing and saluting. The following script requires a Personal Attendant, Lord Chamberlain, Grand Vizier, Senior Flunkey, Butler, Captain of the Royal Guard, Royal Executioner and Junior Satrap.
- Bathsheba's household — a maid, a few supportive friends, baby.
- Nathan — small, serious, determined.
- Nathan's household — noisy, disorganised, hysterical, thoughtless. The following script requires a wife, child, relatives, dogs and donkey.

Script

In Jerusalem it was springtime, the time of year when most kings went forth to fight a war or two. For King David this spring was different. He had sent the army off about a month ago. Instead of commanding it himself, he had given the job over to General Joab. Now he was bored. He paced to and fro in the Royal Palace. He began to wish that he had gone off with the army as he usually did. There really was nothing quite like a good solid war, against old enemies like the Ammonites, Vegemites, or Marmites. He gave a big royal sigh, and decided to do some evening birdwatching from the palace roof. He clapped his hands to summon the Personal Attendant, and then waited while the royal telescope was fetched.

Meanwhile, in a neat little brick-veneer home beneath the palace walls, the lovely Bathsheba was preparing to take a long, luxurious bath. She instructed her maid to fill the roof-top bath, not the indoor one. The maid discreetly whispered in her ear, 'But Madam, the curtains for the roof-top bath are still at the cleaners. Someone on the palace roof could see you!'

'I know', giggled Bathsheba with a sensuous wriggle. Soon the bath was ready, and she climbed the stairs to the flat roof of her home. There in front of her gleamed the bath. Her devoted husband, Sergeant Uriah, had built it for her, just before going off with the Royal Army a month ago. At each corner of the huge marble tub stood a splendid gargoyle. (Move 'human gargoyles' into position at this point.) The arms of the gargoyles supported a roof and rods for side-curtains. Slowly and luxuriously, Bathsheba shed her gown, tossed her hair back, and eased herself into the perfumed waters. Suddenly her maid gave a panic-stricken whisper, 'There's someone up on the palace roof!' Bathsheba smirked and whispered back, 'I know!'

The royal telescope ranged to and fro, picking out pilgrims on the far dusty hills. Their strides lengthened with the afternoon shadows as they raced to arrive before the great gates of Jerusalem slammed shut for the night. Most of the time, however, the telescope was aimed at a modest home close to the palace walls. Then came the magic moment. There was a flurry of activity on the rooftop. The powerful royal telescope zoomed down on the action. The King hunched over the eyepiece, then straightened. He gave a low whistle and muttered, 'What magnificent gargoyles!' He clapped to summon the Personal Attendant, and gave him a hastily scribbled note to deliver. The Personal Attendant woke the Lord Chamberlain and gave it to him. He in turn woke the Grand Vizier, who did the same to the Senior Flunkey, who fetched the Butler, who woke the Captain of the Royal Guard, who kicked the Junior Satrap and told him to deliver the note to the home of Sergeant U r i a h . (Dismiss gargoyles.)

Bathsheba was still brushing her long hair when the maid gave her the note. The astonished maid opened it and read it aloud, 'Why not come up and see me sometime, signed Anon.' Bathsheba smiled an inscrutable smile, and ten minutes later she was gone, her beautiful shoulders warmed by a fur stole that Sergeant Uriah gave her on her last birthday.

She returned home on the following morning. Days of boredom followed. She polished her nails a lot, often looked up at the palace walls, and yawned long yawns. Her husband's letters were boring, and most ended up in the bin after a mere glance. One day it was her turn to write a letter, a letter to the King. Her maid scuttled off after breakfast and took it to the Junior Satrap, who woke the Captain of the Guard, who did the same to the Butler. He bowed and gave it to the Senior Flunkey, and it progressed to the Grand Vizier, the Lord Chamberlain, the Personal Attendant, and then to the King, who was finishing a late lunch. The King sniffed at the perfumed paper, then blurted out, 'Oh, no, she isn't!', but she was, because the note said so. Very awkward for Bathsheba, pregnant, with no husband around the house for two months. Very awkward for a King.

King David tried to arrange a neat cover-up. He had Sergeant Uriah run back to the palace. The Junior Satrap had special orders to meet him and to brush past the snoozing Captain of the Royal Guard, Butler, Senior Flunkey, Grand Vizier, Lord Chamberlain, and deliver him to the Personal Attendant, who gave the sergeant a private audience with the King. Sergeant Uriah was a little puzzled when the King ignored his salute and gave him a big friendly hug. He looked shocked when the King kept pointing to his home, urging him to spend a few relaxed nights with Bathsheba before returning to the war. Sergeant Uriah knew the military rules, and on being ushered out past all the snoozing Royal officials, did not go home, did not pass go, did not collect... Instead, like a good soldier, he spent his nights at the palace guard-room until permitted to leave. He then ran straight back to the battle.

The King scratched his head, pulled thoughtfully on his beard, and made the big decision. He called the Personal Attendant and dictated a note, the last line of which went, '... and so, General Joab, I want you to send Sergeant Uriah out to lead a suicidal attack on the Vegemite fortress.' As we all know, it worked like a charm. Israelite Military Intelligence captured an Ammonite newspaper, and the Personal Attendant gave it to the King as he finished breakfast. The triumphant headline was read out by the King: 'Jewish Spy Caught Between Allied Forces: Sergeant Uriah Dies In Vegemite Sandwich.' 'Ah well,' said the King, burping thoughtfully, ...'you can't make an omelette without breaking eggs.' As he chased the last bits of omelette with the royal fork, he gave these instructions to the Personal Attendant, '... Hmm, put the name up on the honour roll, small wreath at the shrine, usual entry in the paper, and send word to General Joab that due to an administrative error, he won't need to pay any income tax this year.'

Poor widowed Bathsheba! Sergeant Uriah had been a devoted and loyal husband. They had been married for five years. Her friends tried to console her, but she wouldn't listen to anyone, and rushed around packing her bags. After the compulsory seven days of official mourning, she threw off her black clothing, changed into a mini-skirt, and moved into the Palace. Seven months later, she gave birth to a son. She and the King were very happy, and thought that no-one had noticed the whole grubby affair.

They were wrong, very wrong. The same God who made heaven and earth was watching every move they made, just as he always does. God chose his man for the job that had to be done. He picked Nathan, a tough-minded, straight-talking preacher from outside of town. Nathan gazed upwards and gulped nervously as he realised what his job involved. He went straight to his home and saddled the donkey. Whenever God showed him something to do, he always did it fast. His family could see by the look on his face that he had been given another tough assignment. 'Where are you going this time?' they all chorused. 'I am going up to Jerusalem to accuse the King of Israel of murder and adultery' he muttered, and started to ride off. His family, his in-laws, and several small dogs followed him up the hill. He got lots of advice: 'Don't be rash dear, think of your career path!' 'Why ruin your prospects of being Bishop? You'd like being in purple.' 'Why not respect both God and King? Be tactful!' 'We'd hate you to lose your head over this, Daddy!' 'Why take your religion so seriously?' But he rode slowly off to the big city. Meanwhile his wife discreetly checked the death benefits section of their portable superannuation policy.

Nathan presented himself to the Junior Satrap at the Palace Gate. He wouldn't say why he had come, but he looked very serious. He just said that he wanted to see the King. The message was relayed in the accustomed way to the Personal Attendant. He whispered it into the royal ear. The King frowned a nervous frown, then motioned to the Royal Executioner to sharpen the big axe. 'Bring that old religious troublemaker in!' he bellowed. The message was shouted from one official to the other, and finally Nathan appeared, escorted by the entire royal household. Nathan noticed the freshly sharpened axe, the tense expression on the King's face, and the memorial inscriptions praising other martyrs who had performed similar duties. He thought quickly. 'Majesty', he said, 'I come in friendship, to seek your royal advice'. At once the King relaxed, the axe was put away, and the royal servants sat down, leaving Nathan standing in front of his audience. Nathan told his story well, as if his life depended on it. Soon the King was still, listening intently to every word. With dramatic gestures, Nathan told of a wealthy and powerful landowner who received a visitor. Instead of killing one of his own animals for his guest's meal, he went to the poverty-stricken hut of a neighbour, and stole the neighbour's only animal, a hand-fed pet lamb. The King did not wait for the story to end. He stood up, shaking with a terrible rage. His face was purple, his eyes blazed, and his hand flashed to his sword. He roared 'By the Living God, the man who did this deserves to die! Who is he?' Nathan looked straight into King David's eyes and replied, 'You are the man! You stole the lamb of Sergeant Uriah.'

In the silence, Nathan walked quietly out of the room. The King slowly collapsed onto the floor, like a balloon being deflated. When he looked up, the servants were leaving. Soon he was alone. Never had the King felt so alone. The most chilling thought was that he had gone too far this time — that God would never be part of his life again. His voice echoed through the palace as he

ENACTED BIBLE READINGS

prayed a prayer of fear and desperation. 'Wash away all my evil, make me clean from my sin,' cried the King. 'I have sinned against you, and only against you,' he admitted. 'I have been evil from the day I was born, so please forgive me, create a new heart in me.' He concluded with real anxiety in his voice, 'Please don't take your Holy Spirit from me. I know you won't reject a humble and repentant heart.' The King was right. God will not reject the prayer of someone who is flat on the ground, with his royal nose in the dust. King David had to take his punishment, but he was then fully forgiven. God, in his typical way, made something beautiful out of the whole disaster. David and Bathsheba had another son, Nathan was there to celebrate with them, and God loved the little child. He was named Solomon, and became the next King of Israel.

Discussion questions

- Why is a story like this in the Bible? (II Samuel, chapters 11 and 12.)
- Draw up a list of each of David's sins. (Start on the Palace roof.)
- How many of the ten commandments did David break? (Refer to Exodus 20.)
- List every statement about sin, repentance, and forgiveness in Psalm 51.
- Does the teaching in this psalm apply to Christians today?

VARIATIONS

1 As mentioned earlier, this reading can be acted out spontaneously, using the whole audience. Key roles could be assigned only minutes before starting. Those who want a professional result would conduct rehearsals with a carefully selected cast.

2 The teaching point will not suffer if you decide to set this reading in the present day. Substitute 'Mr President' for 'King', and away you go.

3 See Variation 3 of 'The Pearl' for ideas on incorporating direct speech. It is quite easy for the narrator to feed the actors a few lines to speak.

3. The disciples go out

DESCRIPTION

Western Christians have rarely felt comfortable with the 'anti-materialism' passages in the New Testament. This reading dramatises the sending out of the disciples by Jesus, as described in Luke 10:1-12. Matthew and Mark feature similar accounts. The focus is on the importance of trust, and on the virtues of 'travelling light' when engaged in mission. Interest levels are high for all ages, with the humour and updating being aimed at audiences who are overfamiliar with the passage. After some good laughs at the expense of the disciples, the audience has to wrestle with the problem of its own materialistic 'chains'. The question of hospitality, and of support for Christian workers, is also involved. The scene is then set for a discussion which probes the biblical passage and relates it to modern lifestyles.

CHECKLIST

- A copy of the script for the narrator (see Samples)
- A Bible for each participant
- Props and costumes (if desired)
- A copy of the discussion questions for each leader (see Samples)

PREPARATION

1 A simple script and questions are provided, but you may prefer to create your own. Know the needs of your group. Feel free to stretch people a bit, but start at their current spiritual level and move forward from there.

2 Relate your script to the translation normally used by the audience, and ensure that any difficult terms are made clear.

3 Prepare discussion questions at a suitable level, and ask any co-leaders to read through the questions and script with you.

4 Ensure that the 'stage' area is both large enough and visible enough. It must be easy for everyone to hear the narrator.

5 Props are not necessary, but some gigantic suitcases can add to the fun. The contents of the cases can be made memorable, especially if the cast have rehearsed every detail. Note that spontaneous role-playing is equally valid, with only the narrator doing any preparation.

6 Ensure that all participants will have access to a Bible.

RUNNING THE ACTIVITY

This is how the activity might run, involving young teens from a small youth group (20-25 kids).

6.45 Meet with co-leaders, and run through the program again.

7.00 Welcome group members, explain the activity and answer any questions. Provide a 'warm-up' activity if needed. (See page 47.)

7.20 Involving your co-leaders, assign roles to the audience so that all are involved and know what is expected.

7.25 Begin the reading. If some performers are not coping well, they may need assistance from the narrator (repeat a line, emphasise a cue, expand on a description, etc), or co-leaders (acting as prompters, or participating enthusiastically). As narrator, you have the role of 'producer'. Control the process so that the quality is adequate for real learning to take place. Don't hesitate to slow down, stop, or repeat the performance.

7.35 Congratulate the performers on completing

ENACTED BIBLE READINGS

the reading. Form small discussion groups and distribute Bibles. Players should share their feelings about the experience, then read the original Bible passage and wrestle with the discussion questions. All then reassemble for group reports and a summing-up.

7.55 Close off with some prayer and singing.

SAMPLES

Cast

Select and prepare the cast as follows.
- Jesus — firm but caring, knows what he wants.
- Disciples — nervous, excited, inclined to want all the comforts of home, some complaints and whines, but obedient to Jesus. The disciples need to form an open square, so that Jesus can move along quickly, inspecting their bags.

Script

The disciples, all seventy-two of them, were now ready to go out to the surrounding areas. They were to put into practice all that Jesus had taught them. Excitement levels had been at an all time high during their final briefing on the previous night. As they were slipping off home to pack, Jesus had reminded them all to travel light, bringing only what was on the list.

On the following morning Jesus entered the meeting room. It was completely empty. Jesus glanced at his watch, tapped it, and shook it. He gave a long look out of the window, and out of the front door. The disciples were all running late. Not a good starting note for such a big adventure! Jesus checked his watch again, and then cupped his hand to his ear. He smiled. They were coming, chattering away like kids on a school excursion. They poured noisily into the room, each staggering under the weight of an enormous suitcase or pack. They formed a big rectangle, and each dropped their luggage onto the floor with a great thud and a loud sigh of relief. Some had obviously carried their loads for over 200 metres, and looked very tired. The excited chatter suddenly faded as they noticed the serious look on the face of Jesus. There was silence as he stepped forward into the middle of the rectangle.

'It is obvious,' said Jesus quietly, 'that some people here were not listening very carefully last night'. Pacing along the lines of disciples, Jesus wagged his finger at their guilty faces, saying, 'You will need to travel light and fast, telling the good news in many places. I told you that time is limited. I promised that God will provide friendly and generous people wherever you go. Your needs will be taken care of.'

Jesus turned and faced them all. 'Open the bags', he ordered. Silently and meekly, the disciples undid all the locks, catches, straps, zips and drawstrings, until every bag was open. Jesus strode rapidly along their rows plucking out tents, groundsheets, and tarpaulins. The disciples pleaded to have them back, but Jesus piled them up high at one end of the room. Then he spoke to them, 'I told you to enter each new village and find a family who will shelter you. The right household is one which will accept your greeting of peace. The plan is for you to stay in that same house until you leave the village. You are not to take your own house with you!'

Once again Jesus moved along the lines of luggage, and there were more pitiful cries from the disciples. Jesus collected a haystack of sleeping bags, feather doonas, quilts, and travel rugs. He piled them up on the mound of tents and tarpaulins. There were more cries as he confiscated large quantities of biscuits, canned meat, dried fruit, and softdrink. Turning, he said, 'You will stay with the same family for the whole time you are in each village. They will share their blankets and food with you. Some of these families will be generous but poor. If you are later offered better accommodation, you will politely say "no", and stay where you are.'

The disciples groaned a terrible groan as Jesus came along the bags again. There were more cries for mercy, and pathetic excuses, as Jesus pulled out heaps of surplus clothing, portable stereos, extra shoes, and sets of fluffy towels. All this joined the heap at the end of the room. 'You will have to learn to enjoy what your hosts offer you,' said Jesus. 'They will notice what you need, and provide it at their own expense.'

By now the bags looked rather empty, but Jesus started to come along the line one more time. Some disciples fell to their knees begging for mercy as Jesus inspected every wallet. Over the noise of his followers floated the voice of Jesus. 'Keys to one racing camel, voucher for a horse, Bank of Jerusalem Mastercard, two passbooks, tickets for Renta-donkey.' The disciples sat dejected on the floor. Jesus heaped the last of the cards on top of all the surplus clothing. Then he faced them all and explained. 'You are all going out to work hard for the Kingdom. God's people are obliged to look after your every need. Those who reject you will regret it when judgment day comes. Many will listen to you gladly. The harvest is plentiful, but the labourers are few.'

One by one the disciples stood up, looked at their empty bags, and tossed them onto the heap. Then, with growing smiles, they each thanked Jesus, said their goodbyes, and left the room two at a time. Jesus stayed there, waiting for their triumphant return. It was strange, but people on the street that morning said that the disciples seemed to be different people. They had entered the room like tortoises, but left it like athletes going to run a race. There seems to be a moral in all of this. If God tells you to run, then travel light, and trust him. If you are told to stay put, be generous as you look after the runners!

Discussion questions
- Read Luke 10:1-12, Hebrews 12:1-3 and Hebrews 13:1-3. Can you see any connecting ideas? How do these passages relate to us today?
- List the types of Christians who depend on others for their income. (Think of your local church, para-church groups, training colleges, etc.)
- What stops us from being generous with our hospitality and gifts?
- How do we know if God wants us to 'get up and run' for a while?

VARIATIONS

1 Like most enacted readings, this one can be performed by a well-rehearsed drama team or role-played spontaneously by a whole congregation.

2 The script provided features elements from the present era, but could be made consistent with biblical times if preferred. Ensure that the script explains all the cultural terms.

3 See Variation 3 of 'The Pearl' for ideas on incorporating direct speech. It is quite easy for the narrator to feed the actors a few lines to speak.

4 If larger numbers than one hundred are to be involved, modify the script so the families of the disciples stand behind them, giving advice.

4. The exodus

DESCRIPTION

This reading dramatises the key events of the Exodus story (as found in Exodus chapters 1, 12, 14). It makes an effective introduction to this part of the Old Testament (but is also useful for revision). The aim is to bring the pages of Exodus to life and to motivate players to read the biblical account for themselves. Because the emphasis is on experiencing the incident, even the Bible scholars in the group will find it valuable. Participants are able to catch some of the pain of slavery, the joy of freedom, and the excitement of the Red Sea escape. Although this reading could be performed by well-rehearsed experts, it is designed for spontaneous role-playing by the entire audience. Some groups may need a small period of preparation in order to get the special effects just right. The script follows the biblical account closely, but focuses on the most active paragraphs. The additional material links the narrative and stimulates further study.

CHECKLIST

- A script for the narrator (see Samples)
- A Bible for each participant
- A copy of the discussion questions for each leader (see samples).
- Costumes and props (if desired).

PREPARATION

1 A sample script and questions are provided. If you feel they need adaptation, find out the needs of your group. This will mainly affect the discussion process but may lead you to adjust the script. For example, players may need much more background information in order to follow the story.

2 If you wish to create your own script, read the passages through in the translation normally used by the audience. Ensure that the script explains any difficult words or ideas present in that translation.

3 Prepare some discussion questions at a suitable level. Ask any co-leaders to read through both the questions and the script, and to suggest improvements. Produce the desired number of copies of script and questions.

4 Make sure that the stage area is big enough, and that the narrator will be clearly heard. Ensure that all group members will have access to a Bible.

RUNNING THE ACTIVITY

This is how the activity might run if older teens were involved.

12:30 Meet with your team of co-leaders and check that preparations are complete, and that all leaders are clearly briefed.

1.00 Welcome the participants. Explain the activity and answer any questions. Use an overhead projector to give a lightning 'refresher' on the story's details and geographical setting. If the group needs to be 'warmed-up', see page 47. Stress the need for participants to let their imagination flow as they act their roles.

1.20 Using your co-leaders, assign roles and allow time for the different 'teams' to prepare. (See sample script below.)

1.30 The reading begins. Read the script slowly and clearly, watching closely for signs that the players need clearer direction. Ensure that the 'end product' is good enough to drive home your main teaching point. If the standard is low, either pause or repeat the show.

1.40 Form small discussion groups, each led by one of your co-leaders. Allow people to discuss how they felt as they participated. They can

then read some excerpts from the biblical material and tackle the questions. If appropriate, call the whole group back together to share findings.
2.00 Close with music and prayer, following the main theme of God's care for his people.

SAMPLES

Cast

Select and brief the cast as follows.
- Moses — confident, modest but shows normal human emotions (e.g. joy).
- Grumblers — part of Crowd, they are sneaky types who love to whinge and criticise.
- Crowd — respond noisily to main events with fear, joy, despair, etc.
- Egyptian Army — march neatly on the spot, shouldering imaginary weapons (see below.)
- Slave Drivers — lots of whip and abuse; kindness not required (use as army and as 'Egyptians' if necessary).
- Egyptians — stay to one side of stage as a block.
- Pharaoh — arrogant, proud, and loud; uses dramatic gestures.

Script

(Suitable for large numbers, the script assumes that participants have recently done some study on the biblical text, and that the setting is familiar. Cues for the cast are in italics.)

A long time ago, when the pyramids still looked quite new, there was a tribe of foreigners living in the land of Egypt. They were Israelites, and had come to settle in Egypt during a terrible famine in their own land.(*Crowd and Grumblers waved in.*)

They liked living in Egypt, and decided not to go back to Canaan, the land which God had promised them. They built houses and gardens, and had large herds of animals. They had many children, and became so numerous and strong that Egypt was full of them.

Then a new Pharaoh came to power in Egypt.(*Pharaoh and Army/Slave drivers waved in.*) The Egyptian army saluted him. He climbed onto a nearby chair to give a speech. The army applauded. He waved for silence, and began,'People of Egypt, these Israelites, or Hebrews, as some people call them — these foreigners are so numerous and strong that they are a threat to us. If a war started, they might join our enemies and fight against us. They might escape from the country. We must find a way to stop them from becoming even more numerous.'

Pharaoh appointed slave drivers, and sent each one off to choose a gang of Israelites. Each work gang was given heavy work to do. Often they were down on their hands and knees. They had no choice but to obey. Pharaoh looked over the scene of activity and cried out, 'We will crush their spirits with hard labour. Let them build new supply centres for me.' And so the work went on, and on, and on. The cities of Rameses and Pithom were built. When they were finished, the Israelites sat down exhausted to rest and told each other how sick and sore they were. The Grumblers pointed out that God was supposed to be looking after them. They made sarcastic remarks about being 'God's chosen people, living in the Promised Land.'

All this talk stopped abruptly, however, as the slave-drivers had found new work for them. They had to build houses, and work in the fields. Despite all this, the numbers of Israelites continued to increase. All this time, God was getting a leader ready for the Israelites. His name was Moses. (*Indicate to Moses to enter.*) He was an Israelite himself. After getting the best education that Egypt could offer, Moses spent years out in the desert, learning where the waterholes were, and where to find the best paths. When the time was ripe, Moses was sent by God to give the Israelites their freedom. Moses came back to Egypt and found the slaves sitting down exhausted. (*Indicate to slaves to sit.*) As he spoke to them of God's plan, some stood and listened carefully to him. Others sat and showed no interest. The Grumblers muttered noisily, 'All this talk of freedom will just make things worse. The Egyptians will double our work.' Things did get worse. The slave-drivers returned, the Israelites were treated more cruelly, and Moses spent hours in front of Pharaoh, trying to convince him to give the Israelites their freedom. Pharaoh just shook his head, and ordered Moses to leave the room.

Moses went back to the Israelites, who had finished work and were sitting on the ground. He told them to sit in family groups, to eat a special meal, to pack their bags, and to place a special mark on their houses. This mark would cause a deadly plague to 'pass over' their houses, leaving them safe. All the Israelites obeyed him. They sat in family groups, ate the special Passover meal, packed their bags, and put the mark on their doorposts. Then they all went to sleep. The nearby Egyptians all went to sleep too. When morning came the Egyptians woke up and started to scream. Every first-born Egyptian male was dead. No Israelite had died however, because of the special mark. Then the Egyptians knew that God had punished them for their cruelty. They woke up the Israelites and told them to leave the country. The Egyptians even gave them money and food to hurry them along. So off they went, thousands of them. They walked in family groups, and followed the leader that God had given them. They were heading back to the promised land.

Pharaoh called a meeting of all the Egyptians. Standing on a chair, he asked them, 'Where have all our slaves gone?' The Egyptians pointed at the distant crowd of Israelites. 'Oh no,' cried Pharaoh, 'What have we done? We have let the Israelites escape, and we have lost them as our slaves.' He and his officials changed their minds, socks, and underwear. They prepared their finest chariots. (*Players form chariots by piggy-backing others.*) They lined up their army.(*Stand remainder of Egyptians to attention.*) They then set off in pursuit of the Israelites.

Meanwhile the Israelites had arrived at the edge of a great sea. They were exhausted, and sat down to rest. The Grumblers gathered, as they always did. 'We are lost,' they cried, 'are we supposed to swim across or build ourselves an ark?' Some of the Grumblers insisted that it was the Red Sea, others said it was the Reed Sea, and one thought it was the Dead Sea. They all agreed that it looked deep and dangerous. Just as they finished arguing, there was a shout of alarm from the Israelite rear-guard. Soon everyone was screaming in panic, 'The Egyptians are coming to kill us, the Egyptians are coming to kill us!' The Israelites huddled like frightened sheep around Moses, who was standing up on a chair to get a better view of the approaching danger. Most of the Israelites bleated for help. The Grumblers cried out, 'Weren't there enough graves for us in Egypt? Did you have to bring us all out here to die? We told you this would happen! We didn't ask to be taken out of Egypt!' Moses was obviously annoyed. He waved for silence, and the noise died down. He said, 'Don't be afraid. Hold tight, and watch God do the work to save you. You will never see these Egyptians again. God will fight for you; you only need to watch it happen.'

Moses turned, and held his hand out over the sea, just as God had told him to. A great wind started to blow from the east, and soon the sea was driven back. The Israelites watched with amazement. Even the Grumblers watched with mouth agape, though one mumbled that he'd seen it done on a film once. Then Moses led them all off across the damp sand, heading for the oppposite shore. They hurried along, looking over their shoulders at the approaching Egyptian army. Soon they had arrived on the opposite shore, and gathered around Moses. One of the Grumblers smiled and cried out, 'I knew we could do it!' There was a moment of panic amongst the Israelites as they saw the Egyptians cautiously tip-toe onto the sea floor, but the water came back. It came back up to its normal level, and as it rose, the whole Egyptian army sank with a horrible scream.

There was a great cheer from the Israelites, and they carried Moses on their shoulders. But he soon got down, stood on a chair, told them all to kneel, and they humbly gave thanks to God for showing his power and love.

Discussion questions

- Why was God determined to rescue this group of slaves?
- How exactly has God rescued us? Was the Cross really necessary?
- What causes Christians to 'grumble' at God? List the common complaints.

VARIATIONS

1. Though designed for use by the whole congregation, this reading could be performed to an audience by a well-rehearsed troupe.

2. The setting could be updated to the present, although the original is rather hard to improve on!

3. It adds to the performance if lines are fed to the actors. For ideas, see Variation 3 of 'The Pearl' (earlier in this chapter).

5. The lost son

10 - 100   0.5 - 1 hr   10 - 100

DESCRIPTION

This reading forces participants to think carefully about the meaning of a very familiar parable of Jesus. It dramatises what is traditionally known as 'The parable of the prodigal son'. A more accurate name would be 'The parable of the unforgiving son', because the setting (Luke 15:11-32) suggests that Jesus used the parable against a hostile audience of Pharisees. In effect, Jesus likened them to the unforgiving older brother.

The sample script provided follows the biblical text fairly closely, although there are some changes to aid audience involvement. Some 'wrong' endings have been added to shock the audience into finding fresh meaning in an over-familiar story. These endings move the emphasis to and fro, looking at the generous father, at the prodigal son, and at the unforgiving son. The repetition involved is a powerful aid to memory. The scene is then set for some vigorous discussion of the relevance of the parable for modern life.

CHECKLIST

- A Bible for each participant
- A copy of the discussion questions for each leader (see Samples)
- Costumes and props (if desired)

PREPARATION

1 If you wish to create your own script and discussion questions, be aware of the needs of your group. This will affect the wording of both, as well as the endings you choose for the story. Make sure that you 'shock' people into reading the parable with a new enthusiasm.

2 Relate the script to the translation normally used by the audience. Ensure that any difficult terms are explained by the reading.

3 Prepare discussion questions at a suitable level, and then ask your co-leaders to read through both script and questions with you.

4 Ensure that the stage area is both large enough and visible enough. All participants must be able to see and hear the narrator.

5 Props are not necessary, but may be of some value if cultural details need to be explained.

6 Ensure that all participants will have access to a suitable Bible.

RUNNING THE ACTIVITY

This is how you might run the activity with a large church youth group that is over-familiar with the story.

6.45 Meet with co-leaders and run through the program.

7.00 Welcome group members, explain the activity, and answer any questions. Provide a 'warm-up' activity if needed. (See page 47.)

7.20 Involving your co-leaders, assign roles to the audience so that all are involved and know exactly what is expected. If in doubt, get them to practise their actions, noises, etc.

7.25 Begin the reading. If some performers are not coping well, assistance can be provided by the narrator (repeat a line, emphasise a cue, expand on a description, etc), or by co-leaders (acting as prompters, or participating enthusiastically). Remember that as narrator, you have the role of 'producer'. Control the process so that the quality is good enough for real learning to take place. Don't hesitate to stop, slow down, or even repeat the performance.

7.35 Finish the reading by supplying a wrong ending. Let players object to this alteration.

ENACTED BIBLE READINGS

Start an argument by insisting that your ending is an 'improvement' on the original. After some minutes of debate, agree to do the reading again, and offer to correct your error.

7.40 Repeat the reading, possibly moving things along at a faster pace. Provide another 'wrong' ending, and start another argument. Offer to repeat the reading again, and assure actors that you will get it right this time.

7.55 Repeat the reading at a fast pace, and provide yet another wrong ending. After more argument, form small discussion groups and distribute Bibles. Participants now read the original passage, work out why Jesus chose to end his story as he did and wrestle with the discussion questions.

8.15 Call the participants back together, allow for brief reports from groups, and run the reading through with the correct ending. Close with some worship. Focus music and prayers on the main teaching points of the passage.

SAMPLES

Cast

Select and prepare the cast as follows.
- Father — large, dignified, affectionate, with great authority.
- Older son — disciplined, respectful, industrious, self-righteous.
- Younger son — fashionable, fun-loving, lazy, party-goer.
- Servants — obedient, efficient, respectful of Father.
- Swine — on all fours, grunt, feed noisily.
- Party crowd — respond to their cues as follows. *Hard liquor* : drain bottles noisily, wipe lips, toss bottles. *Cigarettes* : inhale luxuriously, then cough horribly. *Dancing* : clap in time as younger son (and partner) skip along. *Boys/girls* : beat chests, flex arms / wolf-whistle, coy wriggles.

Script

There was once a man who had two sons. The older son rose before dawn every morning, and worked hard on the family farm. The younger son was, well, different! One morning, at around 10.30, he got out of bed, went to his father and shocked the household by making a very rude request. He said, 'Father, I want my share of your will now! Why should I wait until you die?' The father called over a couple of senior servants, and together they calculated the value of all that he owned. The final amount was huge. The younger son then demanded his share immediately, and in cash. The older brother jumped up and down in rage, because it seemed that all his hard work was wasted. To raise all this money, animals and machinery had to be sold, and a huge loan taken out from the bank. Soon after, the younger son left for a different land, taking with him all that he had. He did no work at all. He just went to parties with *hard liquor*, *cigarettes*, lots of *boys*, lots of *girls*, and lots of *dancing* (make sure that Party Crowd respond appropriately). Soon, all the money was gone, and the party crowd kissed him good-bye. He was all alone. Hard economic times hit the country. He was hungry. He was so hungry that he decided to work! Work was hard to get, and the best job he could get involved *pigs*. (Give pigs a nod to enter, and a hint to leave, or be silent!) As a Jew, he knew that it was a disgrace even to be near a pig, but he was desperate. Every day he would hold his nose, and go out and feed them seed pods. While the pigs ate, he went hungry. One day he came to his senses. He said to himself, 'I am starving to death! Back home, the servants get more food than they can eat. I am going to swallow my pride and go back to my father!' So he gave a great gulp, swallowed his pride, and started on the long walk home. As he walked he practised his speech of apology, for he knew that he had really hurt his family. He said, 'Father, I have sinned against Heaven and against you. I no longer deserve to be called your son. Please take me back as one of your servants.' He desperately hoped that he would be allowed to meet his father and to apologise.

[Ending one — Angry father]
While he was still a number of hot, dusty kilometres from home, his father spotted him. The father was filled with a burning rage as he thought back over the financial nightmare that the younger son had caused. The father quickly gathered the servants. The older son was called in. Soon the preparations were underway for the arrival of the lost son. The servants put on helmets, belted on their swords, and returned with long spears. The father gave them their orders, 'My older son will take you down to the main gate. You will stand there, shoulder to shoulder, blocking the entrance to the farm. You will not let him through, is that clear?' The elder son, and the servants, nodded enthusiastically. 'Well, what are you waiting for?' growled the father, and the mob were on their way. The younger son was not stupid. Not so stupid that he would miss this sort of message. He could see his old dad standing on the distant balcony. But there was no wave of welcome. Just arms crossed tightly, and a cold, intense gaze in his direction. Just in front of him was the familiar old entrance to the farm. But it was blocked with an armed mob. Soon he could make out the hostile faces of his brother and the senior servants. His pace slowed to a crawl, and he waved his hopes good-bye (wave action). He stopped quite a few metres back from the mob at the

gate, hoping to be able to shout an apology. He got a couple of words out, 'I have sinned', but a hail of well-aimed stones from the servants stopped him. He retreated for about 50 metres, and noticed his father turning his back on him, and walking inside the house. Totally broken now, with all hope gone, the younger son limped away. He knew that he would never enjoy the love of his father again.

[Ending two — The loving older brother]
While he was still a number of hot, dusty, kilometres from home, his brother spotted him. The older brother was filled with compassion for him, and to the amazement of the farm workers, dropped his hoe, and shouted, 'He's back, he's back, my brother is back!' He ran across the field to his brother. He hugged him. He kissed him. He bellowed back to
the servants. 'Bring the horse here at once. Tell my father to prepare a feast! My brother is alive!' While the servants rushed to obey these orders, the brothers had a moment to talk. The older brother listened patiently to the apology from his brother. Then he hugged him saying, 'Yes you really hurt me, and you hurt Dad. But we have been praying together every night for your safe return. Welcome home! We hope you're back to stay.' Then the servants arrived, the horse was brought, the father came out to meet them, and the party lasted for several days. The family was complete again.

[Ending three — The proud younger son]
The journey home was a long one, and as the days rolled past he began to wonder whether an apology was the best approach. Why should he, the brighter of the two sons, have to grovel at his father's feet? He decided to seek shelter at a friend's farm, about a day's walk from home. Using a borrowed typewriter, he prepared a carefully-worded letter. 'Dear Father and big brother,' it went, 'you will be pleased to learn that you will no longer have to struggle away unaided. To help you both run our farm, I have decided to come home for a little while. Please send one of the servants here to collect me. The black carriage will be quite adequate, as I have brought little of my luggage with me.' The letter was hand-delivered, but no carriage arrived, and no letter of reply ever came. The younger son paced to and fro, looking out the window at regular intervals. Other similar letters were typed-up and mailed. Still there was no response. The younger son scratched his head in extreme puzzlement. Finally, deciding that a more humble approach might succeed, the younger son walked home, and arrived in the evening. He met his father and older brother as they rested outside the family home. He got no smiles or handshakes. They folded their arms and just stared at him. The younger son stared straight back at them and said, 'I haven't come here for your charity or pity. I want a job, without pay, as one of your field labourers. I am going to work harder than the two of you put together. I am going to do this my way, and earn your forgiveness.' The father and older brother looked at each other, smirked, and nodded. 'Get yourself a meal down in the servant's quarters,' said the father. 'See you at 5.00 am', sneered the older brother. Then the father and older brother turned their backs on him and went inside.

[Ending four — The original]
While he was still a number of hot, dusty, kilometres from home, his father spotted him. The father was filled with compassion for him, and to the amazement of the servants, ran through the house screaming, 'He's back, he's back, my boy is back!' He grabbed his sandals and walking stick, and set off down the dusty road as fast as he could go. As he drew closer to his son, he became aware of the ragged clothes, the bare and bleeding feet, the haggard face, and the stench of pigs. So he ran up to him and threw his arms around him, and kissed him. The son dropped onto his knees and began his apology. 'Father, I have sinned against heaven and against you. I no longer deserve to be called your son.' But his father would hear nothing of all this. The son was escorted to the house, and the gaping servants were given their orders by the father. 'Quick, prepare a hot bath for him. Go and get a formal suit and all the extras. Get a gold signet ring for his finger, and the best leather shoes for his feet. Bring the fattest and most expensive calf, and kill it for the feast. Set the dining room for a celebration party.' The servants remembered the trouble that the younger son had caused, and just listened in amazement. The father explained, 'This son of mine was dead, but now he is alive again. He was lost, but now he is found.' The servants then got busy, and soon the celebrations were underway. Meanwhile, as the sun set slowly in the west, the elder brother plodded wearily home. When he came near the house, he noticed the lights, music and dancing. He called one of the servants over and asked him, 'What's going on?' The servant excitedly replied, 'Your brother has come back, and your father has killed the fattest calf to celebrate his safe return.' The older brother stamped his foot in rage, and just stood there, with his back to the house, refusing to go in. The servant told the father, who went out to plead with him. The son refused to listen, and replied, 'Look here, all these years I have slaved for you and obeyed every order. You never even gave me a young goat so I could celebrate with my friends! And now this son of yours blows your money on prostitutes, and comes home to get the fattened calf!' The father put his hand on his son's

shoulder and patiently explained, 'My son, you are always with me. Everything I own is yours. But we had to celebrate tonight, because this brother of yours was dead, but now he is alive again. He was lost, but now he is found.'

Discussion questions

These assume that participants are using Bibles.
- List and discuss the sins of the younger son.
- What evidence is there that the younger son understood his failings, repented of them, and wanted forgiveness for each of them?
- What evidence is there that his father missed him badly, and had really forgiven him? In what way is our Heavenly Father like this?
- What was the cultural meaning of the robe, ring, sandals, and calf, all of which were provided by the father? Check in a study Bible, dictionary or suitable commentary.
- What were the faults of the older brother? Why would the Pharisees have been angry at being likened to the older brother?
- What are the precise stages involved in seeking and gaining forgiveness?
- Is it ever right to brush aside an apology, saying that 'All is forgotten'? How do we indicate that we take an apology seriously?
- Should the younger son have rejected 'easy forgiveness', and insisted on earning the forgiveness of his family? Can we earn God's forgiveness?
- If we recklessly damage a Christian friend's possessions, what are our exact obligations to God and to the friend? Must we repair the damage?

VARIATIONS

1 The alternative endings could be performed at daily or weekly intervals, to allow players to reflect carefully on the impact of each new ending. Such reflection will be encouraged if the narrator stubbornly insists that the alterations 'improve' the story.

2 Like most enacted readings, this can be performed by a well-rehearsed drama team, or role-played spontaneously by a whole congregation.

3 There may be advantages in moving the drama into a modern setting, but don't allow this to distract from the 'wrong ending' strategy.

4 The script could be modified to include much more direct speech by players. See Variation 3 of 'The Pearl', earlier in this chapter.

5 If numbers larger than a hundred are to be involved, try using people as extra props. People could form part of the father's flocks, or become poplar trees lining the long drive-way to the farmhouse. There is scope for generous numbers of household servants, party-goers, and pigs.

6 Because the wrong endings require the whole script to be repeated you must beware of boring the audience. A way around this is for the narrator to invite them to learn key sections of the lines by heart, saying them in unison with him or her.

Fourth law of Christian education

'People look after the things they own.'

If participants start to see the activity as something that they have a stake in, their attitude changes. I have noticed that tough and negative youth groups may ignore an adult speaker, but listen attentively to their peers. The lesson is to give significant roles to group members, so that the success of the activity becomes important to them. This works as well with adults as with teens. By building a communal atmosphere (e.g. by using drama) you demolish the 'us/them' barrier.

Sixth law of Christian education

'Aim at nothing and you will probably hit it.'

Few people enjoy aimless wandering around a topic. It is always more satisfying to work towards a conclusion, even if this causes vigorous disagreement. The aim of the activity could be to teach a truth, to shape attitudes, or to improve skill levels. The main thing is to know in advance exactly why you are running the activity. Every educational session should have the needs of the participants clearly in mind. It is an insult to 'fill in time' with purposeless tasks.

Fifth law of Christian education

'Adrenalin is the ultimate appetiser.'

Just as serving the right appetiser can make or break a dinner party, the way to make the simulation (or other activity) really go is to build up the anticipation levels. This can be done through skillful pre-publicity or leaked information. Once you have players' imagination at work before the activity, you can launch the learning time amid high levels of excitement and motivation.

Chapter Five
Drama

'Drama' can mean almost anything!
The term is applied to all sorts of experiences but I will define 'drama' simply as any event where actors communicate a story to an audience i.e. a radio play, a mime performance, a role-play, or a fully scripted stage play. Previous chapters in this book deal with enacted Bible readings and role-playing, both forms of drama; this chapter focuses on scripted plays, narrated mimes and 'spontaneous' plays.

Scripted plays
These are quite familiar to most people. The actors have to learn every word of the script. The advantage is that the actors need not be great thinkers; the writer of the script does all the hard preparation. I have seen raw amateurs communicate with great effectiveness by using good scripts. See the three scripted plays in this chapter for examples of simple, blunt communication. Stage expertise is essential.

Narrated mimes
These often use the stories of the Bible (see chapter four, enacted Bible readings). The one in this chapter is not based on biblical events, but it does drive home some clear Christian teaching. A narrated mime does not require actors to learn their lines. The narrator reads from a script, and the actors silently act out the scenes. Rehearsals are necessary for high-quality results. Mime, if done well, has a unique way of attracting the attention of an audience. I have often noted that rowdy teens tend to chatter away during a play but watch a mime in complete silence.

Spontaneous plays
These resemble role-plays in that actors must adopt a role and respond to a given situation. Rather than a simple scene, however, a spontaneous play may involve a series of complex scenes. The actors need to learn an outline of the action, but there are no lines to memorise — they face the challenge of inventing the dialogue as they go. Because the results are quite unpredictable, this style of drama is best reserved for informal events. If talented hams wish to do a public performance, however, it is worth rehearsing.

Why use drama?
Drama appeals strongly to the imagination. It has all the power of a story, plus the rich stimulation of different voices, costumes, faces, and movement. Despite the increased use of technology in entertainment, the appeal of a live performance remains. In Christian work, drama has been found effective in attracting and holding audience attention. Whether the setting is street evangelism, a youth rally, or a worship service, people stop and listen carefully to drama and they tend to remember its message for a long while. For all of these reasons, drama is a very powerful teaching tool.

If you choose a script which meets the needs of your likely audience and you use enough pace, suspense, and comedy, you will be able to inject a tonne of spiritual input without any audience resistance. You will be able to explore sensitive topics that people normally refuse to discuss. The actors can also benefit. In evangelistic youth work, it may be wise to have a mix of Christians and non-Christians in the cast. The actors can then have some great discussions about the script, and the audience may be more receptive when they see non-Christian friends performing.

Is it biblical?

There are numerous examples in the Bible of the visible acting-out of a message. The disciples were told to remove the dust from their feet (Luke 9:5) as a warning to any town which rejected their message. Ezekiel's enactment of the siege of Jerusalem (Ezekiel 4:1) is another good example. Isaiah 20:2 depicts some daring and sustained acting. The fact that Jesus came in human form and did so many public miracles is evidence that God uses visual communication.

Developing drama skills

Here are some simple and enjoyable ways to help your group develop drama skills. These could be run as a team competition, a warm-up, a serious skills session, or just a relaxed learning time.

1 In private, brief various group members to give short talks to the group on a variety of topics. Record the talks with a video camera and play them back to the group, whose task is to guess what each speakers' instructions were. To help improve performance, the group may offer constructive criticisms.

Each participant will need an instruction card. This will tell them what the topic is, and what their personality is to be. Try some of these:
- Speak passionately about the cruelty of commercialised snail-racing.
- Mumble away, totally bored, as you describe how your bank was robbed.
- Show contempt for your audience as you explain what 'good art' is.
- Sob and sniffle as you describe the tragic death of your pet hamster.
- Have a jealous whinge about the favouritism of the group leader.

2 Give small groups some challenging mimes to perform. As each group performs, the audience tries to guess what the instructions were. These examples would test the skills of most groups:
- You are a herd of camels, drinking at a waterhole.
- You are the Royal Family, sitting in an open carriage.
- You are young children, giving a large Alsatian dog a bath.
- You are car-assembly workers, fitting wheels and hub caps.

3 Form teams of equal size and run a relay race in which competitors mime an occupation to their groups until they correctly identify it. The race could continue non-stop until one team has performed all of the occupations on your list. Examples: nurse, lion-tamer, mechanic, clown, portrait artist, kindergarten teacher, science lecturer, dentist.

When your group is ready to tackle drama proper, choose very simple plays. Miming to a script is a good way to start — see chapter four. Don't be afraid to practise, and to seek critical advice, before performing in public.

How to ruin a drama

Here are a few tips.
- Mumble away at high speed and low volume so your audience can't hear you.
- Keep your back to the audience.
- Avoid showing any emotion as you act — you might wake the audience.
- Glue your feet to the floor; movement might add interest!
- Choose long plays, don't rehearse and fumble key lines.
- Ignore audience tastes and choose scripts because *you* enjoy them.

1. The lifeboat

DESCRIPTION

This little play explores different responses to the message of the gospel. Some choose to decline God's generous offer, and others accept — on God's terms, not their own. While the message is forceful, many in the audience will not grasp it until the play is over, because of the parable format. For this reason, it is important to form discussion groups straight afterwards. If this is not possible, audience members could explore the parable in informal conversation. Experience has shown that teenagers remember live dramas for a long time.

CHECKLIST

- Copies of script for actors and discussion leaders (see Samples)
- A Bible for each member of a discussion group
- Copies of discussion questions for leaders (see Samples)
- Costumes and props

PREPARATION

1 Read through the script with care, noting items that may need alteration. If desirable, re-write the play to meet the needs of your audience. Because youth culture changes rapidly, check that you are up-to-date with any references to fashion and pop music. If aiming at an adult audience, the same degree of cultural relevance is required.

2 Choose your cast, remembering that it may be good tactics to include a mix of non-Christians, new Christians and advanced saints. This measure calms an audience wary of being Bible-bashed, and leads to some great discussions amongst the actors! Experience in acting is not vital, but choose people with loud, clear voices, who are willing to rehearse and to learn the lines.

3 Run a dress rehearsal (with costumes, lights, curtains, and props), and invite some guest critics to come and suggest improvements.

4 When the time comes to perform, allow plenty of time to check lighting, curtains, sound, seating, and costumes. Ensure that those in charge of lights, etc, are well briefed and have a script. Get your cast together early, so that there is no panic. Then enjoy the show.

5 If running discussion groups after the performance, brief the leaders, produce printed questions, and ensure that Bibles will be available for all. If relying on conversations to explore the play, train your leaders by discussing the meaning of the parable, and by anticipating points which the audience might want to discuss. See Sample questions on page 85.

SAMPLES

Props

The 'sea' could be formed by a barrier about waist high. The shipwrecked actors will kneel behind this, with only head and shoulders visible. The 'lifeboat' could be of cardboard, with actors standing behind it. Curtains are optional, but side entrances are useful. If you are able to vary lighting from full lights to 'blackout' it adds impact.

Cast

These instructions relate to the culture of Australian teenagers in late 1984.
Boatman (sunglasses, nautical gear), Muscles (bare arms), Miss Average (bedraggled hair, clothes), Punk (bizarre hair and jewellery), Lazy (as for Miss Average), Trendy (the latest fashions and sunglasses).

Script

Introduction (*Use narrator, taped voice, slides, or overhead projector*)

Once upon a time, the 'Titanic', a huge ocean liner, set sail from England to America. The supposedly unsinkable 'Titanic' hit an iceberg and sank, with few survivors. As the ship sank in icy mid-atlantic, the crew frantically re-arranged the deck-chairs. (*Optional rapid mime of chairs being re-arranged.*) Our next scene shows a lifeboat cruising around looking for survivors. (*Curtain opens, lifeboat moves slowly to centre, rowed by Boatman, Muscles approaches from opposite side of stage, swimming strongly. Boatman stops rowing and leans over the side, obviously concerned and eager to help.*)

Boatman: Ahoy there, come aboard out of that freezing water! I've got a lifeboat here, with lots of room. You can stop swimming now, because you're safe! In you get. Boy, are you lucky that I came along. You would only have lasted a few minutes more in this icy water. Now your life is saved, come on in. (*Reaches out.*)

Muscles: (*Continues to swim strongly.*) No thanks mate, she'll be right!

Boatman: What do you mean, 'It'll be alright?' You're thousands of kilometres from land, there are icebergs, and probably sharks! I can't see any other boats around to help you.

Muscles: No thanks. I don't need anyone else to help me. I can make it by myself. Always have done in the past. I don't want charity. I don't need a crutch to lean on. You go on and rescue people who need your help. (*Shows first signs of fatigue, but swims off.*)

Boatman: O.K., It is your choice. You're free to make your own decisions. If you want to change your mind and get in the boat, this is your last chance.

Muscles: No, I can do it. (*Swims off. Boatman resumes rowing, facing in the other direction. Swimming slows rapidly. Sings line from Frank Sinatra song.*) I did it my way ... (*Drowns.*)

Average: (*Miss Average appears, swimming weakly.*) Help, help.

Boatman: Ahoy there, come over here. I've got a lifeboat with plenty of room for anyone who wants to get in.

Average: Thank God for you. I'd nearly had it. You've saved my life. *Holds up arms, is helped into boat at one end and given blanket.*) How can I ever repay you for what you've done?

Boatman: You can't, it is a gift. But here's a paddle. It'll be good to have you here as a partner. There are so many people out there who need help. Look, there's one!

Punk: Help, help!(*Swims feebly, looks desperate, approaches boat.*)

Boatman: Ahoy there, lifeboat coming. Hang on, we're nearly there.

Average: Erk, look at that punk hairstyle. We're not going to save him, are we? (*Stares, points, looks disgusted.*)

Boatman: We sure are. There's room for all types in this boat.

Punk: Help, quick. I'm nearly frozen! (*Punk holds arms up, Boatman smiles quietly as Miss Average spontaneously stops paddling, pulls Punk in, wraps him in blanket.*)

Lazy: (*Enters slowly.*) Staying alive out here is hard work! (*Swims lazily towards boat.*)

Boatman: Ahoy there, come on in. We've got blankets, food, and hot drinks.

Lazy: Nah, couldn't be bothered.

Punk: Look here, I'll haul you in myself. (*Moves to edge of boat.*)

Average: It's great in here, and worth the effort.

Lazy: No way, you'll soon be asking me to row or something, and I don't want to commit myself. I really couldn't be bothered. I'll just hang around near the lifeboat, maybe keeping one hand on the edge. It pays to keep your options open, because you never know if something better might turn up. (*Clings to one end of boat.*)

Boatman: You don't have the strength to hang onto the edge. You will die. In these conditions you have to get in all the way, or not all.

Lazy: No, leave me be. I know what I'm doing. (*Clings on still.*)

Trendy: (*Enters swimming elegantly, nose in the air, unaware of the boat.*)

Boatman: Ahoy there, come over here, I can save you.

Trendy: (*No reply from Trendy, who looks Boatman up and down, peering critically over her glasses.*) Good grief, can't you afford imported sunglasses? Those things look like 'industrials' from the Apprenticeship Board!

Boatman: (*Friendly grin.*) Never you mind about my sunnies. Do you want to get in and save your life?

Trendy: H'mm, let me look. (*Studies punk.*) Erk, a punk! Punk is about as fashionable as Elvis Presley. (*Swims another stroke, then inspects Miss Average.*) Oh Lord, look at her! (*Boatman turns to look.*) She's wearing a dress from Target! I wouldn't be caught dead sharing a lifeboat with you

DRAMA

	lot. But before I dash, have you got a copy of the current *"Dolly"* magazine?
Punk	Sorry gorgeous, but there's only the survival manual!
Trendy	Oh well, bye bye possums! (*Swims off elegantly.*)
Boatman	It's your life at stake my friend! Come back before it's too late. (*Trendy disappears with horrible gurgle, the imported sunglasses tossed high in the air, caught and worn by the Punk.*) Well, we must keep rowing. There are others out there with no hope unless we get to them. They need us. (*Turns to Lazy.*) Listen friend, this is your last chance to get aboard. Very soon you'll freeze, you'll lose your grip, and you'll drown.
Lazy	No, I'm OK here. Don't rush me. I like to take my time before making decisions. (*Maintains his grip at rear of boat as crew rows in unison, Boat moves off-stage slowly. Lazy lets go silently, obviously having lost all strength.*)
Average	(*Turns, sees what has happened.*) Quick, he's slipped off. Help me, reach out with your paddle. (*Punk helps Miss Average in desperate attempt to reach back to Lazy, now 2 metres behind. Lazy feebly reaches, but can't quite touch paddle.*)
Punk	We warned him.
Average	... But he took no notice. (*Punk and Average resume places and row on, with one last look back at Lazy. Boat exits.*)
Lazy	(*Left alone in mid-stage. Looks weak, tired, scared. Lights dim to 50 per cent.*) Come back, I've changed my mind! (*Silence, no sign of boat, pause. Lights dim further to 25 per cent. Spotlight on Lazy. Lazy turns to audience.*) I think I made the wrong decision! (*Cut lights instantly, hold off until Lazy makes silent exit, slowly bring lights back to normal.*)

THE END

Discussion questions

- As a group, decide what the play was about. Discuss whether it was a useful 'parable'.
- Look at each of the characters in the play (use a spare script). Were they reasonably true to life?
- Draw up a list of images people have of Jesus. The play presents him as a rescuer (saviour), and as a servant. What images does the Bible present?
- Exactly how does God rescue people today?
- Why did the first Christians see Jesus as a saviour?
- Does God give us freedom of choice? Jesus allowed the rich young man to walk away (Mark 10:17-22), but asserts that he chose the disciples (Luke 5:1-11, John 1:35-49, John 15:16).
- Read the parable of the feast (Matthew 22:1-14), noting the fate of those who reject God's generosity, or try to accept it on their terms.
- Why did Jesus tell the parable of the feast?
- Look at the excuses offered by those who rejected both Jesus and John the Baptist (Matthew 11:16-19). Discuss common excuses heard today.
- How would you feel if a loved one rejected a costly present you had offered them?
- How must God feel when people reject his gift of Jesus?

VARIATIONS

1 As mentioned above, the script incorporates a lot of cultural material that dates quickly. This can be varied so the play suits any age-group.

2 If the sinking of the Titanic is a little obscure for your group, re-write the play to revolve around an aircraft crashing into the ocean.

3 If the various attitudes of the shipwrecked persons do not reflect attitudes held by the audience, re-write some lines. The idea is to meet people's needs and to shock them into thinking, 'That's the sort of feeble excuse I often use!'

2. What time is it?

10 - 100   15 mins   6 - 12

DESCRIPTION

This little play lacked subtlety when first performed — it had to! We were a group of strangers, learning to live as a community at a youth camp. Certain people behaved so thoughtlessly that no-one slept on the first night. The next day, three of the victims struck back with this item which unfolded to an astonished lunchtime audience.

The play is so simple that it could be called a skit. It uses loads of repetition and exaggeration to drive home its message that a Christian community can only survive if its members are sensitive to each others' needs.

The blunt message sank home, while the comic exaggeration ensured that everybody had a good laugh. Comedy can sweeten the most bitter of pills. After the performance, there was plenty of time to chat about what it all meant. In other situations, it might be appropriate to hold formal discussion groups.

CHECKLIST

- Copies of script for actors and discussion leaders (see Samples)
- A Bible for each member of a discussion group
- Copies of discussion questions for leaders (see Samples)
- Costumes and props

PREPARATION

1 This drama was tailor-made to meet the needs of our community. You may need to do some 'tailoring' to make it apply to your situation. Read through the script with care, noting items that may need alteration. See Variations on page 88 for ideas.

2 Choose your cast. If the audience is likely to feel that the 'leaders' have hit them with the play, ensure that the cast has a mix of leaders and ordinary group members. Experience in acting is not required, but choose people with extrovert personalities and clear voices who are willing to make fools of themselves, to practise and to learn their simple lines. Note that it is difficult to spoil this play by over-acting.

3 Run a dress rehearsal with props. You need a producer who is willing to make constructive criticisms.

4 The effect is heightened if you present this play with lights dimmed or blacked out.

5 If running discussion groups after the show, produce printed questions, ensure that Bibles will be available, and brief your leaders. See the questions in Samples below.

6 If informal discussion is to take the place of discussion groups, brief your leaders beforehand so that they can anticipate some of the audience's questions (e.g. 'When is bed-time at this conference?').

SAMPLES

Props

Set up the stage to resemble the sort of accommodation your group would use at a residential conference or camp, i.e. a communal single-sex dormitory. Luggage must include lots of noisy metallic objects, and items mentioned in the script (e.g. toiletries, extra clothing). If the stage is to be blacked-out, actors need torches, and a central lamp that can be switched on. Why not add a large wall clock, which a stage-hand can keep adjusting?

Cast

'Jan', 'Jo' and 'Julie' wear summer-weight sleeping

DRAMA

gear. 'The Rest', 3-9 people, wear warm sleeping gear.

Script

Curtain opens to reveal the cast snuggling down into bed. Clock shows 10.30 pm. Lamp is on.

Jan   What time is it? That four-hour bus trip took away all my get-up-and-go! It feels like my bed-time.

Jo   *(Peering at watch.)* It's right on 10.30, Jan. We do the hike to the top of Mount Heffalump tomorrow. *(Yawns, turns to group.)* Is it OK if I kill the light now?

All   *(In ragged chorus.)* Yeah, let's get some sleep. Goodnight!

Jo   *(Crawls out of bed, holding torch. Goes to lamp, switches it off, returns to bed by torchlight.)* Just think, we have to get up at 6.30 am to prepare for the hike. So much for my usual Saturday sleep-in. Goodnight again all.

All   *(In ragged chorus.)* Yawwwwwn, goodnight! *(Silence for a few seconds after all the movement has ceased. Adjust clock.)*

Julie   Are you awake Jo? I can't sleep.

Jo   What's the problem, Julie? I was nearly asleep.

Julie   I can't sleep. I'm just not comfortable. *(Torch comes on.)* The bed feels lumpy or something. *(Torch waves wildly, assorted thumps and bangs.)* I think I'll have to turn the lamp back on. *(Goes by torchlight to lamp, stomping heavily. Lamp goes on.)* Now I can see what I'm doing. *(Looks inside bedding.)* Oh no!

Jo   What do you mean 'Oh no'?

Julie   I've been lying on the chocolates I brought for the hike! Yuk! *(Removes wrappers with great distaste, then licks fingers.)* Oh well, too bad. Better get some sleep I suppose. Goodnight!

Rest   *(Sit up in unison, rubbing eyes, sound annoyed.)* Goodnight!

Julie   Alright, no need to sound so grumpy. It's only ... What time is it Jo? *(Moves over to lamp and switches it off, returns.)*

Jo   *(Fumbles around with torch.)*

Rest   *(Sit up in unison, shine torches at clock, shout in unison.)* It's nearly 10 to 11. How about some sleep! *(Torches go off, people settle, silence for 10 seconds.)*

Jan   *(Bellows)* Ooh, ooh!

Julie   What's the matter?

Jan   I can't sleep. I'm just not comfortable. Now my bed feels lumpy. I think I've been lying on my chocolates. Oh yuk. *(Torch on)*

Julie   Wait a minute, I'll turn the lamp on. Shine your torch over here will you? *(Torch beam follows her noisy journey to the lamp, lamp switched on. Returns clumsily to bed.)*

Jan   Thanks. Hey, it wasn't my chocolates after all. Hooray!

Jo   What was it?

Jan   Only my box of tissues! *(Holds up crumpled remains)* Yawwwn. I'll turn the light off. *(Noisily moves to lamp, turns it off. Returns noisily by torchlight, settles into bed.)* I wonder what the time is?

Rest   *(In unison, as before. Sit up, shine torches at clock, sound annoyed.)* It's after eleven, what about some sleep! *(Same routine of torches off, people settle, 10 seconds of silence.)*

Jo   Ooh, ooh *(Torch comes on.)*

Jan   What is it Jo? *(Shines her torch at Jo.)*

Jo   I can't sleep. I'm just not comfortable. My bed feels lumpy. Maybe I have been lying on some tissues or chocolates. Could you put the light on for a moment?

Jan   OK, just for you. *(Noisily stomps to lamp, switches it on.)* Yawwn, I feel so tired. Can you find the problem?

Jo   Oh how stupid! I left this on the bed! *(Holds up huge boot.)*

Jan   OK, I'm turning the light off now. *(Lamp off, noisy return by torch to bed.)* What time is it?

Rest   *(Familiar routine.)* It is nearly half past eleven! When are we going to get some sleep? *(Usual settling, 10 second pause.)*

Julie   Ooh, ooh!

Jan   What's up Julie?

Julie   My teeth! I forgot to do my teeth. *(Torch comes on, waves about wildly, loud noises of luggage being ransacked.)* I know I packed the brush in here somewhere. Oh look, I did remember to bring the red parka for the hike! Here's the brush and paste. Be back in a minute! *(Noisy stomping exit, tripping over people, etc. Silence for 10 seconds, then noisy return to bed, torch waving wildly.)* I'm glad I remembered. Gosh it must be late. What time is it Jan?

Rest   *(Usual routine.)* It's 11.55 pm, and we want some sleep.

Julie   *(Defensively.)* Alright, alright, I was just doing me teeth. *(Usual settling down, then 10 seconds silence.)*

Jan   Ooh, ooh, ooh. *(Sits up, torch on.)*

Jo   What's the matter, Jan?

Jan   I think I forgot to do my teeth too! Could I borrow some of your toothpaste? *(Both begin a noisy rummage by torchlight.)* Here they are at last! Trust mum to put them inside my bath towel. Thanks for looking,

Jo	but I won't need your toothpaste. Oh that's OK. (*Jo turns torch off, Jan makes noisy exit.*)
Jan	(*After 10 seconds of silence, makes noisy torchlight return.*) Is it ever getting cold out there! Anybody know what the time is?
Rest	(*Usual routine.*) About two hours since we turned the light off!
Jan	(*Snort of disapproval.*) What a cranky lot. Why don't you get some sleep, if you're that tired and grumpy? (*Settling, 10 seconds silence.*)
Jo	Ooh, ooh, ooh. (*Torch comes on.*)
Julie	What's the matter Jo? (*Shines torch at her.*) If you need to do your teeth, you can have my apple. That way you'll shorten this play by about five centimetres.
Jo	I wouldn't mind an apple. Here, toss it over. (*Crash as apple misses, rolls. Search locates it. Noisy munching. Torch off.*) Thanks for that. Cold isn't it? What's the time?
Rest	(*usual routine, sarcastic tone.*) It's only one in the morning! (*Settling, 10 seconds silence.*)
Julie	Ooh, ooh, ooh. (*Torch on, rummaging noises.*)
Rest	Moan, here we go again!
Jan	(*Very loud whisper!*) What's the matter Julie? I think some people are tired and trying to sleep.
Julie	I'm getting cold. I know they said to sleep in a tracksuit, but I always sleep in a nightie at home. What am I going to do?
Jan	You'll have to find a thick pullover and some wool socks. I'll shine my torch while you look in your bag. (*Noisy search.*)
Julie	(*Deafening whisper.*) Got them. Thanks for the help. You can turn your torch off now. (*Blackness.*) It must be nearly two am.
Rest	(*Usual routine, mimic of loud whisper.*) It is nearly 2.00 am. (*Settling, silence for 10 seconds.*)
Jan	Oooh, oooh. (*No torch, but noisy movement.*)
Rest	(*Sound very weary.*) Moan.
Jo	(*Shines torch.*) What's up?
Jan	(*Hoarse whisper.*) I'm getting cold. My warm clothes must be out in the other room. I've got a rug here, I think. Shine your torch here a minute. (*Noisy struggle.*) I can't see what I'm doing. Could you quietly put the light on, just for a second?
Jo	OK. (*Very elephantine tip-toe across to lamp. Turns it on.*)
Rest	(*No movement at all, but hum Brahms 'Lullaby' at gradually increasing volume until rug is found. Humming stops.*)
Jan	Thanks Jo, you can turn it off now. (*Lamp off, all settle, usual ten seconds silence.*)
Rest	(*In the darkness.*) Haven't you forgotten something Jan?
Jan	Eh? What are you talking about?
Rest	OK team, one two three! (*usual routine, bellowing!*) Three am and all is well! Only four hours to breakfast. (*Silence.*)
Jo	(*After usual 10 second pause, begins a noisy feast by torchlight. Sounds of potato chip packets, biscuit tins, soft drink.*)
Julie	(*Hoarse whisper.*) Hey, what's up?
Jo	I'm starving, probably because I got cold putting the lamp on for Jan. What's the time?
Rest	(*Usual routine*) About three crisps past four! Chomp, chomp. (*Silence, 10 second pause.*)
Julie	(*Loud whisper, torch waving.*) Hey Jo, wake up, wake up.
Jo	(*Loud and sleepy.*) Arrh, what's the matter?
Julie	I can't get back to sleep. Want to get up now?
Jo	Yawwn. Ohhh OK, but let's keep it quiet. People might be sleeping. (*Torches wave wildly, noisy dressing process. Clumsy exit, a few seconds of silence, then footsteps return from a great distance. Another torchlight rummage.*)
Jan	Hey what's up?
Jo	Quiet! (*Changes to noisy whisper.*) We were going to get up, but it's still dark outside, and really cold. So we're getting back into bed again. (*Noisy struggle to get back into bed. Torches out. Usual long silence.*)
Jan	Are you sure it was still dark? It must be...
Rest	(*Usual routine, but fast enough to interrupt.*) Nearly five!...
Jan	I think I'll get up now anyway, now that I'm wide awake. I know where I can get a warm fire going. Going to join me?
Julie	No, we'll have a snooze here until the alarm goes at 6.30.
Jan	(*Dresses, noisy exit with departing whisper.*) See you later. (*Silence again, then noisy returning footsteps. Tip-toes last few steps. Torch used, sound of bodies being shaken. Whispers.*) Hey you two, get up! The sunrise is great. It's a big orange ball over the ocean! Get up, it's ...
Rest	(*Routine, interrupting.*) ... Nearly six. (*Silence for 10 seconds.*)
Jan	(*Shrugs, exits alone, silence.*)
Julie	Come on Jo, it's getting light now. It

DRAMA

	must be...
Rest	(*Lightning response.*) Just after six.
Jo	OK, let's get up. (*Two dress noisily, but without speaking, exit with exaggerated tiptoe action.*)
Rest	At last! (*Total silence for 5 seconds, then gentle snores for another few seconds. Alarm clock goes off loudly.*) Groan!
J, J, J	(*Jo, Jan, Julie return and stand at door. Cheerily call out in unison*) Come on, up you get. We're going on the hike today! How come you all look so tired?
Rest	(*Sit up in unison, point, shout out-*) Because of you!
J, J, J	(*Indignant, point at themselves.*) Cos of us?
Rest	(*Throw up hands in horror, lie back, then pop up in turn, each mimicking some of the evening's interruptions. Lights come on.*) I'm cold, I can't sleep, where's my toothbrush, what time is it, quiet or you'll wake them up, where's my jumper, the sunrise is great... (*Close curtain.*)

THE END

Discussion questions

- Read Ephesians 4:1-6, 25-32; 1 John 3:16-24; James 1:123--27, 2:14-17, and 3:17.
- Based on the above, draw up a list of vital qualities for Christian groups.
- Relate these standards to practical matters, such as rosters, duties and giving.
- Why does the Bible see the quality of our daily living as so important?

VARIATIONS

1 This script concerns sleep at a residential event, but the broad issue is that of respect for the needs of others. You could use this basic structure, but change the details to cover problems faced during worship, discussion groups, planning meetings, etc.

3. Cross for sale

DESCRIPTION

With a cast of only two, and a handful of easy props, this drama is within the reach of any group. It looks at the burden of human sin, and at the freedom that Jesus offers. The significance of the Cross in Christian belief is covered from a number of angles; the emphasis is on discipleship, while 'cheap salvation' is discouraged. The lines need to be memorised, but are 'short and sweet'.

The play is light, visual and witty, but because of the serious content, it is essential to allow generous amounts of time for teaching and discussion. This applies to groups of mature saints as well as to non-Christians.

CHECKLIST

- Copies of script for actors and discussion leaders (see Samples)
- A Bible for each member of a discussion group plus pens and paper
- Copies of discussion questions for leaders (see Samples)
- Costumes and props

PREPARATION

1 Read through the script with care, making any changes that are necessary to meet the needs of your audience. Note that a change from pack/rucksack to suitcase is not recommended, because a suitcase is not such a good visual 'burden'. However, you should feel free to mention other 'sins', and to promote other aspects of discipleship.

2 Choose your cast with care. The play is so short that a few mumbled lines would destroy its effectiveness; the use of gesture and facial expression is also important. (See notes in the script.)

3 Put plenty of time into rehearsing, and invite some critics along to provide constructive advice. Ensure that the dialogue will be clearly heard.

4 The play should be followed by teaching and/or discussion. These will require careful preparation, such as the printing of questions. See Samples. Leaders of discussion groups should be prepared — give them copies of the script and the questions and time to work out answers to likely questions.

5 Ensure that all members of discussion groups will have access to a Bible.

SAMPLES

Props

- The 'burden' could be a large rucksack or backpack, loaded with heavy parcels. You could use bricks — cover them with paper and mark different 'sins' on each. One line in the script requires the customer to have some long thermal underwear in a pocket of the rucksack.
- The cross should be as tall as the salesman and made of two planks, secured only with cord or elastic straps. It should be clearly possible for the customer to separate the two pieces and walk off with only one of them. Four signs are attached to the cross, preferably at the ends of each plank, and bear the following messages in large print:

> Tell other people about Jesus; Keep Jesus as your best friend; Be a generous and loving person; Put God in charge of your time and money.

Attach a large price tag to the cross, proclaiming the following:

DRAMA

> **$$$$ PRICE $$$$**
> Price paid in full, by the death of Jesus on the cross. Available free, so you can afford it. Carry it with pride!

Cast

The Customer can wear normal clothing. The Salesman needs gloves (concealing 'scars' marked on both palms), and might want to wear a white coat to symbolise purity. If you want a vigorous audience response, appoint a prompter, who carries large placards bearing the words — 'No', 'Yes', 'Go back'.

Script

This was produced for a family worship service in a suburban church. The drama was followed by a sermon which explored the main teaching points. S = salesman, carrying cross, C = customer, carrying pack. Stage directions are in italics.

S (*Enters from rear of hall, moving down aisle to front, calls out to audience repeatedly*) Cross for sale, cross for sale. Going free, going free, in exchange for heavy loads, free exchange for heavy loads! Have you seen anyone carrying a heavy load lately? Have you seen anyone struggling with a heavy load? Look, here comes a customer!

C (*Wearily appears at rear of hall, plods exhausted towards Salesman at front, stops beside him.*) This pack weighs a ton, and it gets heavier every day! I really can't cope with such a heavy load.

S (*Carefully leans cross against some furniture, then turns to inspect the pack.*) You're right, it does weigh a ton. What have you got in it? (*Pulls out some heavy objects and reads labels*) These feel like bricks, and your pack is full of them! Here's a label: 'January 12, 1979. Lost my temper at a workmate. No apology given.' Look at this one, 'March 10, 1987. Cashier gave me excess change. Didn't correct mistake'. Here's another, 'December 25, 1990. Felt deep anger and jealousy over presents given to my sister.' Why are you carrying all this stuff?

C Well there's nothing I can do about it. Like everyone here, I keep on sinning, and I have to carry the load of guilt around for the rest of my life.

S But the load is going to get heavier every year. Imagine the weight by the time you're 65! Every sin here feels as heavy as a brick. You'd have to be 'a couple of bricks short of a load' (*gestures to indicate mental deficiency*) to keep on like this. What's this doing in here? (*Pulls out long thermal underwear from pack.*)

C They came free with the pack, and they're supposed to be flame resistant.

S Yes, you'll need them where you're bound. Look, you seem to be getting a rather grim deal out of carrying this great pack of yours.

C Ah, but there are benefits. With this on my back, I can blend in with the crowd anywhere, even with people in this audience! Anyway, that's enough about me. What are you doing here?

S I'm here to make you a really good offer. If you buy this cross, I'll take away that heavy load of yours. (*Presents cross to customer.*)

C Hmm, here's the price tag. Hey what's this all about? (*Reads it aloud.*) 'Price paid in full by the death of Jesus on the cross. Available free, so you can afford it. Carry it with pride'. Wow, this looks too good to be true. Wait a minute, there's some fine print on each arm of the cross. (*Reads each notice aloud, slowly and carefully.*) 'Tell other people about Jesus, be a generous and loving person, keep Jesus as your best friend, put God in charge of your time and money.' (*Turns to audience*) Well, I like the idea of getting rid of this load. What if I dump my load and just take part of the cross? Is that fair enough? (*Invites audience to agree, but Salesman shakes his head to indicate 'No'. Prompter likewise stirs up audience to cry 'No'.*) (*Customer to audience.*) You mean I have to carry it as it is? (*Audience encouraged to chant 'Yes'.*) Blow that! I'm better off carrying this pack. No deal. I'm leaving! (*Begins to exit, but audience begs him to 'Go back', and Salesman beckons him to return.*)

S Come back, you might not get a second chance. (*Customer reluctantly returns, now looking very weary, scratches head thoughtfully, starts to loosen pack.*) You'll have to kneel to get rid of it.

C (*Obviously reluctant.*) I'm too proud to kneel for anyone! (*Thinks a moment*) Alright, I'll kneel if it means that the load is gone forever. (*Kneels, pack is removed and put to one side by Salesman.*) But what happens to the pack? Won't it turn up again later on?

S Oh, I'll take that down to 'Trinity Waste Disposal Centre', and it will be completely and permanently destroyed.

C Won't that sort of service be expensive?

S Yes it was, but I'll just take off these gloves (*displays bare palms*) and show them the marks on my hands. There will be no extra costs.

C Well, thank you. This hasn't been an easy decision, but I'm sure you've changed my life forever. (*Looks cheerful, energetic.*)

S I certainly have. Goodbye. (*Waves as Customer exits, then faces audience.*) You know, I thought he wasn't going to take it for a moment. It's amazing how many stubborn people there are in the world. (*Shoulders pack, exits bent over with its weight.*)

THE END

Discussion questions
- Using pen and paper, describe what the death of Jesus on the cross was all about. Try to express it in a hundred words or less.
- Read about the scapegoat in Leviticus 16:20-22. Compare this with Isaiah 53:5-6 and with Hebrews 9:27-28, looking for common ideas.
- This offer to remove all our sin and guilt seems too good to be true. How do we pay for it? Read Ephesians 2:1-10.
- How can we live so as to show that God is in control of our lives? Ephesians 5:1-21.
- Why do so many people believe that they should carry some (or all) of their guilt around on their shoulders?
- What is your response to this claim, 'To insist that Christ cannot forgive your sin, is to insist that he be nailed up again on the cross'?
- Is being a 'disciple' only for elite believers? Read Matthew 28:16-20.

VARIATIONS

1 As mentioned above, you may vary the cultural trappings to suit the background of the audience. Remember, however, that the burden must be 'attached' to the person in some way, to symbolise the grip of sin on a person's life. You could adjust the notices on the cross to describe other dimensions of discipleship, but make the replacements equally weighty.

2 You may prefer to give the play a shock ending where the customer refuses to accept the costs of commitment. This may hit home at

4. Ben David's store

10 - 100   0.5 - 2 hours   8 - 30

DESCRIPTION

This is really an improvised or spontaneous play. The actors study an outline of the story, and then enact the key scenes. It is simple enough for inexperienced teenagers, but adults could also do it.

The story is set in a small country town. A worker runs into financial strife, turns to crime and finally faces total ruin. A rescue offer comes from an unlikely source. The drama is a parable of Christ's rescue mission, and takes many viewers by surprise. It is especially potent for evangelism. Actors and audience alike are drawn powerfully into the emotions of the story. They will remember the parable and its meaning for a long time.

Run as a learning exercise for the cast, the whole exercise could occupy a couple of hours; if they were to perform it to an audience, the scenes could be acted out in a few minutes. Either way, it is essential to allow time for reflection and discussion.

CHECKLIST

- Copies of story outline for actors and discussion leaders (see Samples)
- A Bible for each member of discussion groups
- Copies of discussion questions for leaders (see Samples)
- Costumes and props

PREPARATION

1 Read through both the story outline and the scene instructions. Make whatever changes to cultural content, or even the teaching points, as are necessary to meet the needs of those involved.

2 Choose the cast with care. It may, for example, be wise to give some key roles to non-Christians, particularly in youth work. It would be good tactics to give a non-Christian the role of Ben David, because that role forces the actor to imagine being a Christ figure. See page 54 for an explanation of role-reversal. For a public performance, ensure that actors have loud, clear voices, and are willing to rehearse.

3 Distribute copies of the story outline and scene instructions for them to study.

4 If a public performance is planned, have a dress rehearsal using any planned props, costumes, etc. Invite some critics along to offer constructive advice.

5 Prepare some good discussion resources for use by small groups after the performance. See Samples. Brief the leaders of discussion groups, and ensure that all participants will have access to a Bible.

SAMPLES

Props

None are essential, but you could add atmosphere to a public performance by setting up appropriate backdrops.

Cast

Varies according to each scene, but the full line-up is as follows.

- Fred: likeable Mr Average, works for local council as gardener.
- Jane: ambitious, sharp-tongued, honest wife of Fred.
- Kids: of school age, upset by it all.
- Boss: manages all the Council staff; sly and powerful.
- Banker: Sly and powerful, controls the only bank.
- Judge: visits town monthly; stern, fair, and aloof.
- Ben: honest, fair, manager of the only supermarket.

- Cop: strict, fair, and honest; the senior policeman in town.
- Friends: nice people, but unwilling to give help when needed.

Costuming is optional, but worthwhile for a public performance.

Outline of story

Once upon a time, around 1990, in the quiet country town of Hogsville, there lived a gardener named Fred. He was married to Jane, and had two school-age children. He worked for the local Council, mowing lawns and tending the plants in the park. One day his Boss at the Council had a phone call from a needy relative who was unemployed. He decided to give a job to the relative, but then realised that the Council budget would not support an extra gardener. The Boss called Fred into the office and gently explained that times were hard, and that he (the Boss) had just been told to sack one of the gardeners. The Boss offered to write Fred a reference if he needed one, and despite Fred's pleas, gave him the sack.

Fred went home to explain this disaster to Jane, who was furious. Jane had always wanted Fred to improve his qualifications. Now their house was at risk, because they had a big loan from the bank to repay. As Fred went to ask the Banker for advice and help, a vital phone conversation was taking place. The Banker had unwisely lent out huge sums to some business friends, who now could not repay it as soon as expected. The Banker was trying (in vain) to recover one of these loans before the Head Office noticed. Then poor Fred entered with his tale of woe. The Banker saw his chance, and explained that Fred's home would be auctioned if any payments were missed. This would solve the Banker's problem.

Soon the family finances were in chaos. Despite Jane's nagging, Fred found no work. Welfare payments didn't cover the bills. Jane was too proud to ask for help from the Salvation Army, or from their friends. One day, when the Banker threatened to sell the house, Fred just 'snapped'. Clumsily disguised, he went and robbed the town's supermarket. For a day or two the family could pay its bills, but the owner of the supermarket, Ben David, and the local cop were soon knocking on the door. An irate Jane and two hysterical children watched Fred being taken away.

When the Judge came on his monthly visit to town, he listened carefully to the list of charges being read out. The Cop and Ben David told how Fred had terrorised the check-out girls and run off with thousands of dollars. The Judge explained to Fred that he understood the pressures that led to the robbery. He also explained that the law must be obeyed, and that he had no choice but to declare Fred guilty and punish him. The sentence would be a fine of $100,000 or 10 years in gaol. When Fred begged for mercy, the Judge agreed to leave Fred in the police lock-up until the following month. This would give Fred time to raise money to pay the fine.

Weeks passed, and Fred begged his visitors to help him. His friends made sympathetic noises, but were unwilling to part with their hard-won savings. They did offer to keep an eye on the kids for the next ten years however. Jane came to inform Fred that she was about to sell the house and go back to her mother. One day Ben David came to the police station to see the Cop about a licence, and overheard Fred's conversation with a visitor. Ben heard Fred say that the thing he most wanted was to be able to walk back into the supermarket, apologise and refund the money.

A month passed, and a packed courtroom heard the Judge explaining the fine to the accused. Fred sadly declared that he had not been able to raise the fine. Just as the Judge was about to pass final sentence, and send Fred to gaol, there was a cry from Ben David. Ben stepped forward with a briefcase. The crowd gasped as they saw Ben count out $100,000, and pass it over to the Cop, who checked it. The crowd knew that this was a very costly gift. The Judge smiled, and asked Fred if he wished to accept this generous offer. Dazedly, Fred accepted the gift, and was escorted out of the court by Ben. Fred offered to pay back every cent, but was firmly told that it was a gift. Ben then asked Fred to report to the supermarket next morning, to work as one of the delivery drivers. As they walked off, Fred was still making silly statements about planning to 'pay him back', and Ben was still firmly explaining that it was a gift of love. They both looked very happy.

Scene instructions

The story could be acted out in four scenes. Try this framework:

Scene one
Fred goes off to work, the Boss gets the phone call, Fred is sacked, Jane is furious, the Banker uses the phone, the Banker fails to help Fred.

Scene two
Financial strain, help not asked for, robbery, money again, arrest by angry Cop and Ben.

Scene three
Judge hears all the evidence from Cop, Fred pleads guilty, Judge explains the law, offers time to raise money, Fred visited in Police cell, friends won't help, angry Jane visits, Ben overhears a conversation.

DRAMA

Scene four
Judge explains penalty choice, declares Fred's guilt, begins to pass sentence, Ben interrupts. Fred accepts offer, exit.

Discussion questions

- Draw up a list of characters in the story, listing their faults. Rank them from 'most evil' to 'least evil'. Compare and discuss lists.
- Read James 2:8-11. Can Christians rate others on how evil they are?
- Could the Judge have handled things differently (assuming that the penalties mentioned were then in force)? Was he a good Judge?
- Read through Romans 2:1-16, 6:23 for a few tips on how God judges us.
- Note with care the generosity of Ben David in the story. Discuss the real costs involved in the fine payment and in the job offer.
- Skim through one of the Gospel accounts of the punishment handed out to Jesus (e.g. Mark 15), and note the cost involved.
- To refuse a costly present is both foolish and dangerous. Note the warnings in John 3:16-21, 12:44-50.
- Draw up a list of good reasons for ignoring the gift Jesus offers. Try!

VARIATIONS

1 If it will make the exercise more effective, change the location and time-setting of the story.

2 If it will make the teaching point more memorable, vary the response of the main character to Ben David's offer (e.g. from full acceptance to partial acceptance to full rejection).

3 To involve more people, have a completely separate cast for each of the four sections. This would provide roles for up to thirty people.

5. Gratitude

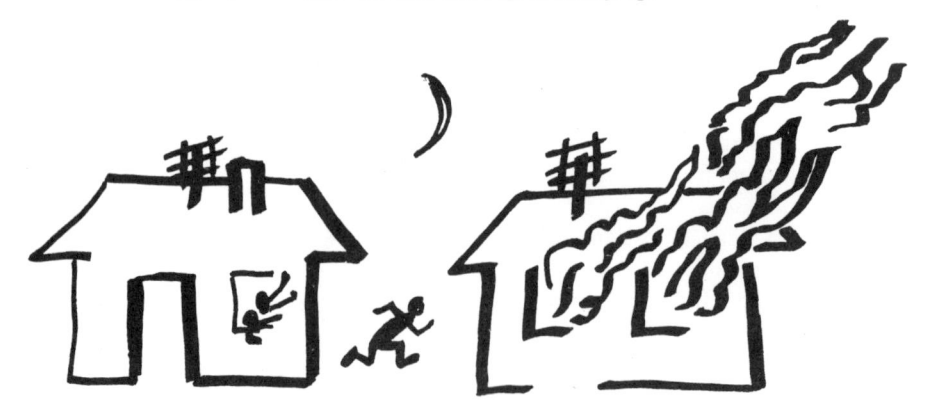

DESCRIPTION

This short and hard-hitting narrated mime could be used for discipling mature believers, or for communicating to the unchurched. The play is set in modern-day suburbia. In it, two families behave very differently. One represents human selfishness and ingratitude, while the other demonstrates God's generosity and love. This extreme contrast is designed to make audiences reflect on their own 'casual' response to God.

The painful truths are softened with humour, so that audiences will want to follow the story all the way to the closing line.

Because the drama is a parable, and not all viewers will understand the hidden meaning, it is essential to have a short talk or discussion before or afterwards.

CHECKLIST

- Copies of script for actors and discussion leaders (see Samples)
- A Bible for each member of discussion groups
- Copies of discussion questions for leaders (see Samples)
- Costumes and props

PREPARATION

1 Read through the script with care, noting items that may need alteration. If necessary, re-write sections of the script to make the scenes of family life more familiar to your audience. You may also need to make the parable more (or less!) difficult to understand.

2 Choose your cast, either using existing families, or creating families by conscripting individuals. Avoid type-casting i.e. do not choose ultra-pious folk for the Christie family, and immature Christians for the Everage clan. The drama can be performed solely as a mime, so the cast do not need great speaking ability. There is however, scope in the script for the cast to be fed a few key lines. (If you do this, ensure that the actors can be heard clearly.)

3 If possible, create some simple stage sets and arrange appropriate props. Some creative miming will suffice if resources are limited.

4 Run a dress rehearsal (using any lights, sound systems, props, and stage sets) and invite some guest critics to offer constructive advice.

5 Whether the parable is to be unravelled before or after the performance, ensure that the speaker or discussion-leaders are properly briefed and have copies of discussion questions. Ensure that group members will have access to Bibles.

SAMPLES

Props

A backdrop of two typical family homes could be made from cardboard. This should match up with the 'fire' scene. A bicycle, building supplies and clothes-line are useful if available.

Cast

The Everage Family comprises father, mother, son (12 years). The Christie Family comprises father, mother and son (9 years). Mrs Everage is dressed very elegantly. The other actors and the narrator should wear neat casual clothes.

Script

Once upon a time there were two happy Forest Hill families. The Everage family had the compulsory 1.9 children, a large mort age, a gleaming white car, and a mother who did the laundry, cooking and gardening in high heels. Their neighbours, the Christie family, had a cute baby and

DRAMA

a nine-year-old son, Christopher. The Christie family were very generous neighbours, often helping the Everages when they needed a hand.

For example, one Saturday, young Everage junior was struggling away with his 12-speed twin-turbo gee-whizz BMX bike. Young Christopher Christie heard the noise, and the language, and offered to help, saying; 'It will only take half an hour to tighten up those parabolic oscillators on the front shredder.'
(Christopher *'it will only take half an hour to tighten up those things.'*)

Meaning by those things the parabolic shredders on the back oscillator, of course, and behold, it was just as he had said, the oscillators were soon shredded, and Everage junior muttered a brief thanks...
(*Everage junior 'Thanks'*)

And rode off, as the sun set slowly, and majestically, in the west, like it always did in those parts.

Later in the week Mrs Everage was out struggling with a heavy load of washing, still wearing her cocktail frock and high heels. Mrs Christie yelled out 'Do you want a hand?'
(Mrs Christie *'Do you want a hand?'*)

'I sure do', said Mrs Everage.
(Mrs Everage *'I sure do.'*)

Because Mrs Everage seemed so depressed and tired, Mrs Christie stayed until all the washing was hung on the line, and then helped with the ironing and some heavy cleaning. As Mrs Christie left to do her own housework, Mrs Everage gave her a big hug and said,
(Mrs Everage *'You've been very kind.'*)
... or something like that.

Next weekend Mr Everage was having a bit of trouble repairing his garage roof, which leaked every time it rained. Come to think of it, it could hardly leak any other time, could it? Without bothering to ask if he was needed, Mr Christie wandered over with some of his building tools and helped to rebuild the roof. It took the two of them about ten hours, but Mr Everage said 'It won't leak again for a long, long time — perhaps until the politicians take a pay cut.'
(Mr Everage *'It won't leak again, ever. Not in a million years.'*)

It wasn't long after this that the fire happened. While the Everage family slept, one of their seven electric toothbrushes had a short circuit, setting the bathroom ablaze. Soon the whole roof was a mass of flames. The Christies saw what was happening, and while Mrs Christie rang the fire brigade, Mr Christie dashed into the smoke to save the family. He staggered out with the Everages' average 1.9 children, went back for Mrs Everage, and pushed her out a window. He returned into the roaring fire to get Mr Everage.

Minutes later, Mr Everage squeezed out of a small window on the other side of the house, just as a large section of the ceiling collapsed. Mr Christie did not come out. His body was found later by the fire brigade and police.

The Christie family found life hard without a Dad. They didn't have much time to feel sorry for themselves, however, because they offered to share their home with the Everages until the builders fixed the fire damage. Soon the Everages were back in their own home, and their life returned to normal.

For the Christies life wasn't quite normal. Money was tight with no weekly pay-packet coming in. Mrs Christie was offered some weekend casual work, but needed a free baby-sitter. She asked Everage Junior if he could help for a couple of hours. But he said 'No, I get lots of homework in grade six, and in the afternoons I have to watch lots of videos of a Gothic-punk Christian music festival.'
(Everage Junior *'No, I get too much homework.'*)

Mrs Everage couldn't help, because she always rested on Saturdays, so that she could look her best on Saturday night concert outings.
(Mrs Everage *'Sorry, but I always rest on Saturdays.'*)

Mr Everage was annoyed at being asked. He snarled back at Mrs Christie, who was almost in tears by now, 'Can't you see?'
(Mr Everage *'Can't you see?'*)

'I'm still trying to repaint all the rooms damaged by smoke from the fire,' he added.
(Mr Everage *'I'm still trying to repaint all the rooms damaged by smoke from the fire!'*)

As Mrs Christie sadly walked away, he shouted after her, 'I suppose you'd forgotten all about our fire?'
(Mr Everage *'I suppose you'd forgotten all about our fire?'*)

But Mrs Christie didn't reply.
(*All cast to freeze for 5 seconds, then exit.*)
THE END.

Discussion questions

- Think back over the drama, listing examples of the help given to the Christie family by the Everages.
- List ways in which the Christies helped the Everages.
- What was the cost to the Christies each time they helped?
- Was it fair for Mrs Christie to ask for some help with baby-sitting?
- Had Mrs Christie forgotten about the smoke damage from the fire?
- How could the Everage family have shown some gratitude?
- How generous should the Everage family have been to Mrs Christie?

- Why should gratitude be part of our response to God?
- Specify how God has shown generosity towards us.
- Read Romans 5:6-8 and Ephesians 1:4-8 to glimpse Paul's gratitude.
- Read Luke 7:36-50 for a story concerning faint gratitude. Can any human really claim to 'have been forgiven little'?
- Imagine coming before an awesome and holy God, and having to watch a video replay of every ugly thought, word, and action from your life. What sort of defence would you offer?
- Read Luke 17:11-19 for the story of one leper's deeply-felt response. How does the story reveal the intensity of his gratitude? Why would the healing have meant so much to him in that society?
- To get some idea of our debt to God, read Matthew 18:23-35 for the story of the unforgiving servant. Convert the amount of gold into ounces (one talent = 75 pounds, one pound = 16 ounces), and multiply by the current gold price (e.g. $500/ounce). The idea of the servant repaying a debt of this size is both tragic and comic. Do we hold fantasies of being able to 'pay our way' into Heaven?
- Why then should Christians be a loving and a forgiving community?

VARIATIONS

1 As mentioned earlier, you may need to change the cultural setting from urban to rural, or similar, to make the story more relevant to the audience.

2 If you have specific local needs in mind, replace paragraphs from the sample script with scenes reflecting the 'ingratitude' of your target community (e.g. slack worship or greed).

Chapter six
Board games

Not board games!
Some people would say that the name of this activity is better spelt 'bored games'. The name conjures images of wet afternoons, crumpled cardboard boxes, trivial questions, the rattle of dice, and artificial laughter. You can indeed run board games at that level. Alternatively, you can devise board games which are intellectually demanding, emotionally challenging, or riotously funny. Read on to discover the enormous potential of this teaching tool.

How many types are there?
The limit is set only by your imagination. It is up to you to create an appropriate game. Most games use a simple playing board which has a long line of squares. Players move small tokens from the starting square towards the finish. The pace of movement depends on points earned by answering questions, performing tasks, or rolling dice. This mechanism has a hidden value which is explained below. The obvious focus of the game is the set of tasks or questions. There is no limit to the quantity or quality of these tasks or questions. They can be aimed at university professors or at young children. The questions might deal with party politics, Bible knowledge, Christian ethics, social involvement, or family life, while performance of the tasks may mean some costly physical actions. Competition can be between individuals or teams.

What is the value of the board?
This is a good question. Why not keep the questions and throw away the board? The answer is that the board is a valuable distraction which greatly lowers the threat level of the activity. Many players would not cope with an oral examination on their religious beliefs but feel safe with a board game. Often there seems to be a 'gentlemen's agreement' that the focus is on the little tokens moving around the course. In reality some significant learning and sharing goes on.

What about answers to the questions?
To provide answers to the questions, the following systems can be used.
- Group members can vote to indicate whether an answer was correct.
- You could provide a set of 'answer' cards to be consulted after a question has been attempted.
- A panel can provide answers at the end of the game session.

Individual counselling or a formal lecture, might be the way for your group to conclude a game. Note that board games can be used not only to teach, but also to revise, test, provoke, but motivate, and to draw out opinions.

But Christian belief is more than a set of facts, isn't it?
The board game format is often used to explore a collection of facts. This is not however the only option. The traditional 'question card' can be replaced with a 'set task' which the whole group must perform in close co-operation. Your task or questions could involve elements of value clarification, simulation, or role-playing. See other chapters in this book for explanations of these. For example a player might pick up a card, read out a complex case-study, and then have to 'solve' the problem.

Equipment

1 The typical playing board is up to a metre square, made of paper or cardboard, and marked out with a line of 20-40 squares. This line may have a clearly marked 'start' and the squares may be large enough to contain a token for each player. The board may need to have some clearly-marked areas for the placement of question cards etc. All this assumes that about four to eight players will use each board. That is the most common number. If you are planning to involve 30-40 people with each board, make it huge. The opposite applies if the game has to fit on small coffee tables. Here is a sketch of a typical board for 4-8 players. It is cheap, portable and disposable.

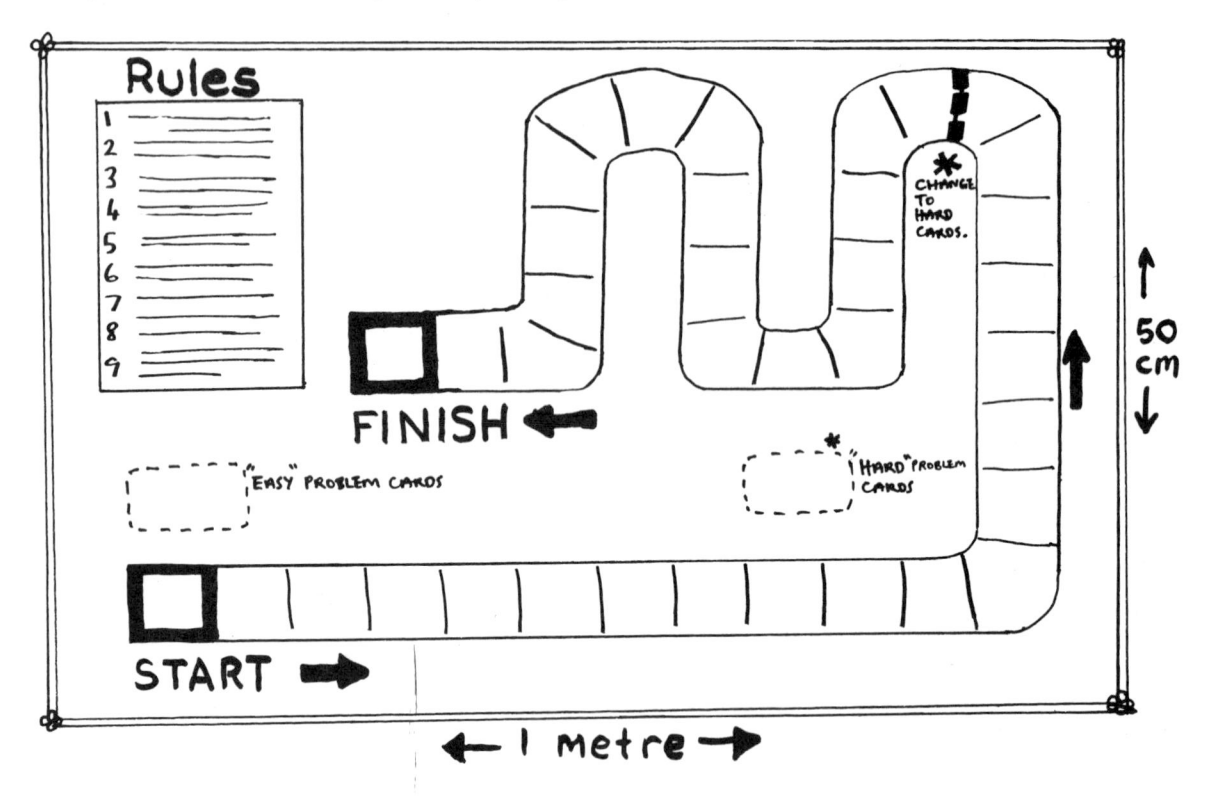

Note that there is no law limiting your creativity in the area of board design. One group used the carpet squares of a dining hall, and had human tokens to measure each team's progress. It was quite spectacular.

2 Arrange a supply of small, movable objects for use as tokens. Try using pebbles, pieces of carrot, clothes pegs, buttons, wrapped sweets, keys or coins. You make these tokens highly symbolic, e.g. use coins if the game is about money, or pieces of vegetable if it is about starvation.

3 A simple way to produce your own question cards is to write or (type) the words in eight compact little paragraphs per A4 page, and to photocopy the required amount before cutting into rectangles measuring 10 x 7 cm. These slips of paper can be used as they are, or made durable by gluing them onto light cardboard or small blank cards, both available at newsagencies. To use the cards provided in this chapter, enlarge by 33% (using a photocopier), for a size equivalent to that mentioned above.

If you find yourself constantly making minor changes to your set of question cards, try storing the words in a word processor or a computer. This way you can keep your original set of questions and produce a modified version whenever needed.

4 The games in this chapter each feature some system to determine how far each token moves. If you plan to modify these games, or to build your own, here are some tips on the movement of tokens.

- Players can roll a dice, move forward to the appropriate square, then read out the questions allocated to that square. There need not be any movement in relation to how well the question is answered.
- Players can choose a card, perform the task then find out from the umpire (or a score card) how far to move the token.
- After listening to a player's answer, team members can vote to indicate how far the token moves. A common method is to vote simultaneously, indicating +1, -1, or 0 by holding thumbs up, down or folded in.
- If anonymity is desirable, players can drop matches into a voting box according to an arranged system (e.g. no matches means agreement, one means unsure, two means disagreement.)

1. Saint of the century

18-100   1 - 1.5 hours   8 - 80

DESCRIPTION

This challenging game aims to help players discover how much, or how little, they know about their faith. When playing it at leadership conferences, players have discovered large gaps in their knowledge, and the result has been record sales of study Bibles, handbooks, Bible dictionaries and commentaries. Embarrassment is minimised by keeping the pace hot — players get only a minute to answer each question.

A group of players gather around the playing board, placing tokens at the start. They then take it in turns to pick up a card, read out the question, and try to answer it. A quick vote decides how far the player's token moves; there is no time for debate. When the game is over, some visiting or resident 'gurus' are asked for their opinion on the more controversial questions. By the end, players discover that they know more than they thought they did. The game tends to boost their confidence and encourages them to keep growing.

CHECKLIST

- Playing boards, counters and question cards (see Samples)
- Copies of the rules for each leader and each playing group
- Book stall or resource display
- Copies of discussion questions for each leader (see Samples)
- Copies of question cards for panel members

PREPARATION

1 Read through the list of sample questions. Delete any that do not relate to the planned audience and add a few that cover current hot issues. The idea is to make the game meet the needs of the players.

2 Show your list to your co-leaders and invite comments. If you can, skim through a list of likely players, ensuring that all will be able to participate fully. Discuss possible problems with the co-leaders.

3 Prepare sets of question cards, playing boards (with about thirty squares on each), tokens and any other requisites. If you plan to have a panel session to wind up the game, ensure that panel members have plenty of time to read through their own copy of the questions.

4 Check that the playing area is large enough. It should be reasonably comfortable and sheltered, and could be outdoors. (Note that violent wind gusts will cause havoc.) Players could sit at tables or on the floor.

5 If you plan to have a book stall, ensure that quality reference books are stocked. You could ask your co-leaders to guide players in their purchases.

RUNNING THE ACTIVITY

This is how the game might run at a training event for youth leaders:

1.00 Gather co-leaders for a final briefing. Set up the playing area.

1.30 Invite players to enter the area, explain the game and its rules and deal with any questions. Form small playing groups and let them begin.

1.45 Along with any helpers, move around quietly, ensuring that groups play at a brisk pace and follow the rules.

2.30 Check to see if groups have had enough. If so, close the game, form discussion groups and ask players to refer any controversial questions to a panel of experts.

2.50 Defuse any resentments by pointing out that you deliberately chose very demanding questions. Encourage use of the book stall, and dismiss players for afternoon tea, vigorous theological debate and free time.

3.00 Note that leaders should be alert at this time. There may be players who need help with book stall purchases, and others who feel a bit fragile and demoralised. Watch especially for lone 'heretics' who felt somewhat rejected by their groups - they will need both sound teaching and warm friendship.

ESSENTIAL RULES

1 A playing group must have four to eight members, each of whom selects a token and places it on the 'Start' square. One or more players should act as time keeper.

2 When asked to begin, the player with the darkest eyes is to select a card from one of the piles and give it to the player on their left.

3 The person receiving the card has 60 seconds to read it aloud to the group, ponder and give an answer. The group is to remain silent while this happens. When the answer is given, or when the timekeeper announces that time is up (whichever is the sooner), the group votes.

4 The voting system is as follows. The timekeeper calls for a vote. The other players should simultaneously present their right fist. Each thumb pointing up indicates agreement; thumbs down means disagreement; and thumb folded means 'no vote'. Each vote has a value of − 1, 0 or +1. The timekeeper adds up points, and the token of the person who answered the question is moved. Note that the token must be moved backwards if the point score is negative.

5 The person who has just answered the question is to choose a card and pass it to the left. The game continues as above.

6 Note any controversial matters and save them for the panel discussion at the end of the game. Do not bog down in debate during playing time.

SAMPLES

Questions

These questions were designed to challenge mature Christian youth leaders, aged 19-30 years. You could place them (each on a separate card) in five distinct labelled piles on the playing board.

Category A — Basic Christian beliefs
- Describe the status of Scripture.
- What is Heaven?
- Who is the Holy Spirit?
- What does discipleship involve?
- What is Hell all about?
- How important is social justice?
- What is the connection between good works and salvation?
- What should baptism involve?
- Describe the character of God.
- Why was Jesus both human and divine?
- What is the significance of the Cross for the church today?
- Why is the 'empty tomb' considered so important in the New Testament?

Category B — Christian ethics
- Give a Christian perspective on slavery.
- Why does the Bible oppose adultery and premarital sex?
- Is the Bible too hard on homosexual behaviour?
- How should Christians respond when the poor are oppressed?
- Should a Christian police officer fire her revolver at a dangerous criminal?
- Should a Christian be involved in a nudist colony?
- What is the Christian view on pleasure?
- Should the Church actively condemn gluttony and materialism?
- Are all addictive substances off limits for true believers?
- When may a Christian serve in the armed forces?
- Is it wrong for a Christian to grow rich through hard work?

Category — Know your Bible
- Explain the names of these books: Luke, Titus, Revelation, Acts.
- What is the main message of the Song of Solomon?
- What relevance does Genesis have for us today?
- Summarise the events described in Exodus.
- What happened in the time of the book of Judges?
- What do Paul's letters reveal about his character?
- Describe Paul's contribution to New Testament theology.
- Why is the book of Acts so special?
- Describe the 'radical' message of the minor prophets.
- What was the main warning given by Isaiah and Jeremiah?
- Why was the book of James almost thrown out of the Bible?
- What controversies caused Paul to write to the Corinthians?

Category D — People in the Bible
Briefly explain the life and importance of:

BOARD GAMES

- Adam and Eve.
- Abraham.
- David.
- Nathan the prophet.
- The disciple Peter.
- Joshua.
- Mary, the mother of Jesus.
- The Assyrians and Babylonians.
- John the Baptist.
- The apostle Paul.
- Bathsheba.

Category E — Life in Bible times
- What did a crucifixion normally involve?
- Describe the impact, for a Jew, of contracting leprosy.
- What was the common belief about demon possession?
- What did it mean to 'go the second mile'?
- Who were the Samaritans?
- What was the Jubilee originally meant to involve?
- What was it like to be conquered by the Romans?
- Describe some of the highlights of Greek culture.
- What was strategic about the time and place of Jesus' birth?
- Describe or sketch the route followed by Moses in the Exodus.
- Describe or sketch the main physical features of Palestine.

Discussion questions

- Which of the above questions would you like to refer to the panel?
- What category of question did you have most trouble with?
- Do you feel motivated to improve your understanding of your faith?
- What can Christians to do to improve their spiritual knowledge?
- What are the 'essential ten' Christian resource books to have on the shelf?
- Describe the features of the ideal study Bible.
- When is it really handy to have a good knowledge of the faith?
- What courses exist for Christians who want to learn more?
- What daily disciplines keep a Christian growing in the faith?
- Describe the impact of a mature Christian you know.

VARIATIONS

1 For younger players, answers to questions could be provided by a resident umpire, or read from an official answer sheet.

2 Questions could be classified according to difficulty, and players given the choice of easy/medium/advanced piles.

3 Players could choose their own cards, rather than having them chosen by a neighbour.

4 Children as young as ten could benefit from this game if the questions and rules were adjusted. See Variation 1 above.

2. Truth or dare

13 - 21   1 - 1.5 hr   8 - 80

DESCRIPTION

Designed to meet the needs of an exuberant youth group, this active game can serve as a very effective get-to-know-you game; it also frees players to state their religious beliefs. This makes the game an ideal tool for informal evangelism. Players take it in turn to deal with the cards on the playing board. The 'Truth' cards force them to share some personal thoughts with their fellow players, while the 'Dare' cards involve horrific penalties and embarrassing assignments. The final result is very pleasing to all concerned — the 'Dare' cards provide loads of entertainment, while the 'Truth' cards help players discover some of their friends' deeper beliefs and values.

It has been interesting to note the 'crowd-pulling' nature of this board game. One school-based Christian group ran it as an evangelistic venture, and had to turn away dozens of kids. The room was overflowing. When run with a staid youth group, the game broke down all barriers, setting teenagers free to express what their faith really meant to them. Perhaps the best clue to the game's impact is the fact that players rarely remember who won or lost, because of the excitement of learning more about other people.

CHECKLIST

- A playing board, copy of the rules, set of cards and tokens for each group (see Samples).
- A box of resources for carrying out Dare penalties (see Samples)

PREPARATION

1 You need to know the needs of the playing group. With these needs in mind, go through the list of Truth and Dare cards. Delete those you don't want, and create relevant and up-to-date ones. Dare cards should not be excessive, but they must be intimidating enough to encourage the use of the Truth cards.

2 Show your draft list to your co-leaders, and discuss it carefully. Note any Dare penalties which may require adult supervision. It is usual to place a leader with each playing group, for both control and ministry reasons. Such leaders must know the exact aims of the activity.

3 Produce playing boards which can serve 4-8 players each, and which have about 30 squares between 'start' and 'finish'. Supply tokens, cards, and a set of rules for each board. Set up a resource box filled with items needed for the Dare activities.

4 For a playing area you need a reasonably comfortable and sheltered space, either indoor or outdoor. Beware of wild wind gusts causing chaos. Messy penalties could take place just outside this area if necessary. Players could sit around tables or on the floor. You may need to be able to address the group both before and after the game.

5 Whether the aim is to 'get-to-know-you' or to evangelise, conclude the game with a suitable activity, e.g. conversation over the supper table, followed by a well-aimed talk. To capitalise on the achievements of the game, it is essential to plan your concluding activity carefully.

RUNNING THE ACTIVITY

This is how the game might be run with teenage evangelism in mind. The players could range from youth group leaders to 'fringe' members with little church contact. See Variations for ideas on adapting the game to suit other age-groups.

BOARD GAMES

1.00 Gather co-leaders for a final briefing. Set up the playing area.
1.30 Invite players to enter the area Explain the game and is rules and deal with any questions. Form small playing groups with one leader in each, and let them begin.
1.45 Along with any helpers, move about quietly, ensuring that groups play at a steady pace and follow the rules.
2.30 Check to see if groups have had enough. If so, close the game. Allow time for packing up, then call players together and announce the next activity.
2.45 Give leaders plenty of time to chat with players who have indicated some spiritual need. This opportunity to discuss personal beliefs is too precious to waste. A relaxed coffee-break might be the best method.
3.20 Close off with a challenging talk which encourages players to continue in their spiritual journey. Make it clear that help is available for those who wish to talk further, receive a Bible, etc.

ESSENTIAL RULES

1 Each playing group must have 4-8 members, a board, one token for each player, and two sets of cards (marked Truth and Dare). Each group should appoint someone with a watch to act as timekeeper.

2 Players select a token each, and place them on the 'Start' square. The player with the longest eyelashes begins, by choosing either a Truth card or a Dare card. If a Truth card is chosen, the player may reject it and go for a Dare card. A Dare card may not be rejected.

3 The player must then read the card aloud to the group. If it is a Truth card, the player has 60 seconds to read the card and give an honest answer to the question.

4 The other players vote in unison, at the command of the timekeeper, to indicate whether they feel the answer was sincere or not. To vote, players present their right fist with thumb up (= +1) or thumb down (= -1). If the vote is positive, the player's token moves forward according to the total voting score. If the result is negative (e.g. -3), the token moves backwards (three spaces), and a Dare card must be tackled.

5 Once touched, a Dare card may not be returned. The penalty must be paid in full.

6 A soon as the first player has handled a card, and the token has been moved, the person on their left has a turn. Continue this clockwise pattern around the group until playing time expires.

SAMPLES

These cards were designed to meet the needs of a teenage youth group. The game served both as a 'ice-breaker' and as an aid for conversational evangelism. The playing boards had about 30 squares, and had marked locations for the two stacks of cards.

Truth cards

- How would an atheist (who believes there is no God) decide whether something is 'fair/unfair' or 'good/evil'?
- What convinced the disciples that Jesus had risen from the tomb?
- If a person is a Christian, how do they stay a Christian? Give six practical ideas.
- How often should a Christian read the Bible? Explain.
- Describe the contents of the Bible, and your attempts to read it.
- Recite the famous verse found in John 3:16, and explain what it means. If you don't know the verse, borrow a Bible and read it out.
- How can Christians feel sure that God will accept them if they die tonight?
- What is the difference between 'getting done' and being baptised?
- What effect has this youth group had on your spiritual growth?
- Describe your favourite memory of primary school religious education, or of Sunday School.
- Tell the group what your religious beliefs are. You have only 60 seconds.
- Do you think that a person can be both a good scientist and a Bible-believing Christian?
- Who is Jesus Christ?
- What would change if you became a more active member of this church?
- Does becoming a Christian mean giving everything up?
- Describe your feelings when you attend a communion service.
- What holds you back from exploring Christianity more deeply?

Dare cards

(Most involve getting supplies from the central resource box.)

- Bring back one litre of water and drink it in 60 seconds, while the others tell you jokes.
- Do 50 star jumps, stopping after every ten to yell, 'Time flies when you're having fun'.
- Comb the hair of six people in other groups (avoiding those you know well), saying apologetically, 'I'm sorry, but I just can't help it.'
- Stand on a chair and sing a favourite song at full volume for 30 seconds. Your group will applaud.
- Blow up a balloon until it explodes in your face. Group members will make funny faces at you while you perform in front of them.

- Blow up a balloon to full size, tie it, then sit on it until it bursts.
- Use the lipstick to paint your nose bright red. Leave it on until your next turn.
- Ask your group members to decorate your face with shaving cream. You may remove it after doing a tour of every other group, asking them to look at you.
- With help, stand upside down and drink a glass of Coke.
- Go to the far corner of the room, stand on a chair, and do farmyard noises for 30 seconds at full volume. Your group will applaud.
- Go to the oldest person in the room and flatter them for 30 seconds commenting on their grooming, dress sense, sophistication and style.
- Go to the second oldest person in the room, remove their shoe, sit on the floor at their feet, and improvise a phone conversation with the Fairy Godmother for 30 seconds. You must then put the shoe back on.

VARIATIONS

1 If closer control of the Dare penalties is desirable, appoint a 'Lord High Executioner' to supervise all penalties.

2 Given tight controls, and appropriate new cards, children as young as ten could gain from playing this activity. Adults can also enjoy it, provided that you create new cards.

3. Hot spot

DESCRIPTION

This game was created to help Christian students (aged 11-18 years) at secondary schools. Players sit around a board and select question cards, which describe some of the problems that they face as Christians at school. Each player in turn must read out a 'dilemma' and respond quickly. The others immediately vote to indicate their approval or disapproval and the players' token is moved forward or back in response to the voting result.

The game appears competitive, but the progress of the players' tokens is merely a formality that helps reduce anxiety. Later, group discussions may be held on the more controversial topics.

CHECKLIST

- Playing boards, cards and tokens for each group (see Samples)
- A copy of the questions for each leader (see Samples)
- A copy of the rules for each group and each leader (see Samples)

PREPARATION

1 Read the list of sample questions. Delete any that do not relate to the needs of your players and add new ones that helpfully cover the latest issues.

2 Show your modified list to your co-leaders, invite them to add their own improvements and seek agreement as to what the 'correct' answers might be.

3 Prepare sets of question cards, playing boards (with about 30 squares on each), tokens and a set of rules for each board. Your assistants should have a copy of the rules, and possibly the questions as well.

4 Check that the playing area is large enough. Players need to be sheltered from wind while seated around the playing boards. They also need to be able to hear any opening or closing remarks from the organisers.

RUNNING THE ACTIVITY

This is how the game might fit into a brief school lunch-break.

1.00 As soon as the bell goes, set up the room with playing boards, etc.

1.05 The moment you have four players, explain the game and allow them to start. Repeat this pattern with the next dozen or so players.

1.10 Latecomers are placed with existing groups, who allow them to join in and explain the rules to them as they go.

1.15 All players are now involved in a game. Leaders move about, providing help where needed. Play continues at a rapid rate.

1.30 Announce the close of play. Ask groups to nominate the hardest questions. Meanwhile one leader should walk around collecting the playing equipment. Explain that next week's meeting will deal with the hard questions from the game.

1.45 Close the meeting with your usual announcements, worship, etc.

ESSENTIAL RULES

1 Each playing group must have 4-8 members, all of whom select a token and place it on the 'Start' square.

2 To begin, the player with the longest hair picks up the top card, reads it aloud to the group, and then answers the question, all in 60 seconds.

3 One player must act as timekeeper,

107

announcing when the 60 seconds has expired and calling players to vote. This is done by placing right hands on top of the timekeeper's hand. A hand placed flat is a positive vote and a clenched fist is a negative. Add up the votes and move the player's counter to its new position.

4 Repeat this pattern, moving clockwise around the circle, so that all players have the chance to tackle some cards. Do not get bogged down in noisy debate; the 'controversial' questions will be tackled later.

SAMPLES

Questions

These were designed to meet the needs of urban secondary school students, aged 12 to 18 years.

- One of your friends, a 'born loser', is very sensitive to criticism. During cooking class, she produces a truly awful cake. She asks you to taste it and comment. What do you say?

- You make a joke which deeply hurts another person's feelings and they walk off, obviously upset and angry. The rest of the group just shrug their shoulders and mutter, 'What a grump'. What do you do?

- A few Christian students in your school want to revive the lunchtime Inter-School Christian Fellowship (ISCF) meetings. You know that your friends would laugh themselves silly if you attended. What do you say to the Christian students?

- One of your friends arrives at school, silent and red-eyed. The rumour is that his father died on the weekend. What could you do?

- Your friends start talking behind the back of one group member, saying that his mother has a boyfriend, and that divorce seems inevitable. The comments are basically true. Should you say anything?

- Your weekend away with the church youth group went well On Monday morning, some of your 'tough' friends are boasting of their colourful exploits. Do you tell them what you did, or stay quiet?

- Your friends are having a vigorous discussion of religious beliefs. One claims to believe in God, but insists that 'good deeds' are the way to get into Heaven. Because the rest of the group claim to be atheists, you are reluctant to attack the only other 'believer'. What do you say?

- One of the toughest and nastiest students in the school is sitting alone. Her face looks bruised and swollen, and she has been crying. What can you do?

- One of your classmates invites you home for the weekend and the family tries hard to make you feel welcome. You discover that the evening 'treat' is a trip to the drive-in theatre to see a film that you know is a disgusting R-rated one. What can you do?

- You accidentally notice that a friend in your class is being sold illegal drugs by some older students. Your friend begs you to keep quiet, and the drug dealers hint at what might happen if you cause trouble. What should you do?

- You are one of the best athletes in your class, but always avoid fights. After school there is an ugly scene when a student your size tries to provoke the class midget into a fight. Your response is?

- Your teacher is a person you greatly respect. His valuable pen is stolen by a thief in your class, and you see it happen. What do you do?

- Your school is on fire. Your class has been moved to the oval and told to stay put, but one of your classmates is missing (probably developing photos in the darkroom.) Do you rush back into the burning building to save your friend?

- A Christian friend has at last found true romance and appears to be very happy. The beloved, however, is a committed atheist and this worries you. How should you act?

- You are being picked on by a big student in your form. You discover that this bully has a father in gaol, and is trying to keep it secret. How will you respond?

BOARD GAMES

- Your close-knit group of friends are sitting in the middle of an empty oval, talking. They start telling jokes which become very crude. You would look silly if you walked away. What can you do?

- One of your classmates, fiercely proud of her ethnic background, reeks of garlic. Others refuse to even sit near her. Should you say something? What do you say?

- A friend's family are going through hard economic times, but proudly try to keep up appearances. Your friend's clothing is not warm enough for the winter cold, and his lunch is miniscule. What action would be appropriate?

- You are part of an elite hockey team, and are preparing for a vital game in the series. The coach, who is famed for winning trophies, openly instructs three of the players to use 'dirty' tactics, which will injure opposition players. Can you do anything about it?

- The annual class party is coming up soon. The host, a popular classmate, announces that his parents will be out for the night. Other students grin, and tell of wild sexual romps at similar events. What should you do?

- Helping with the Christian club at school is eating into your study time. Do you continue as a key leader, and watch your marks drop?

- The Christian group at your school is boring. The student leaders lack courage, humour or imagination, and the speakers are worse. What can you do about it?

- You do well at school because you put in long hours at your homework. A friend, who is starting to drift further and further behind, asks you to spend an hour or two per night, helping with revision and homework. You would love to help, but are committed to hih personal achievement. What should you do?

VARIATIONS

1 Question cards could be classified according to age-levels, degree of difficulty, or even gender.

2 Questions could be adapted to meet the needs of other specialised groups (e.g. young apprentices, senior clergy).

3 The game could be kept as is, but played with the parents of secondary students. It would help them understand the reality of school life. This strategy is linked to that of 'role-reversal' as described on page 54.

4. Boama village

DESCRIPTION

On the surface this looks like a very simple board game. It is best played as a competition between rival teams, each with their own board. The teams hurry through the problem cards, desperate to finish first. When the game is over, a startling discovery is made: the teams with the slowest times appear to have scored the most points. What can be behind this mystery?

The answer lies in the upside-down values of the kingdom of God and the richly person-centred culture of Boama village. Solutions which lower the dignity of human beings are of little value to these gentle people. In contrast, Western culture worships time, money, and efficiency. When the scores are added up, decisions which reflect Boama culture are rewarded with bonus points, while hasty 'Western' solutions earn no points.

This board game has a strong 'simulation game' flavour. You may want to refer to chapter two, which tells you how to get the best value from that sort of activity. To fully exploit the learning potential allow about 50 per cent of the time for the 'competition', and the remainder for a carefully planned discussion, which should include some Bible study and quiet reflection.

CHECKLIST

- Problem cards, score cards and a copy of the rules and a playing board for each group (see Samples), plus a pen and some tokens for each group.
- A Bible for each participant.
- Written instructions for each judge.
- Copies of the rules and discussion questions for each leader (see Samples).

PREPARATION

1 Read through the Sample problem cards on page 113 and 114. With the group of players in mind, delete unsuitable problems and replace them with more relevant ones.

2 Show the list to your co-leaders, inviting constructive criticism. Discuss the purpose and the mechanics of the game and ensure that all leaders fully understand the rules and have copies of the discussion material. Appoint a couple of leaders to serve as judges.

3 Prepare problem cards, score cards, judges' instructions, players' rules, playing boards, pens and tokens.

4 Check that the playing area is suitable. Players need to be able to sit around the playing boards, using either tables or the floor. You must be able to address the whole group at the beginning and end of play.

5 Ensure that all players will have access to a Bible during the final discussion.

RUNNING THE ACTIVITY

This is how the game might run if played with young adults who are mature Christians and are of at least average educational standard. The pace might be slower, and the content simpler, if less capable players were involved.

2.00 Final briefing of leaders and judges. Set up the playing area. Place problem cards face down on the boards, and in correct numerical order. (Card one must be on top.)

2.30 Welcome players, explain the game and its rules, then deal with any questions. Form playing groups of equal size, assign them to locations, and give them time to get organised

BOARD GAMES

and to study the playing board. When all is set, give the signal for the first card to be inspected. The game has now started.

2.34 Along with other leaders, move quietly around the groups, helping them to follow the rules. You could also subtly encourage speed and aggression.

3.05 By now, a couple of teams may have finished. You may want to allow the 'slow' teams time to complete some more, or all, of the cards.

3.15 Declare the game finished. Collect all score cards and give them to the judges for processing. Ask players to assemble in a compact circle for a group discussion (see 'How to debrief' on page 12).

3.20 During the debriefing, discuss players' experiences and explore possible answers to problems.

3.30 Ask the judges to announce the scores for speed of completion, and then to announce final scores. When the uproar has died down, explain how important matters of culture and faith are to the Boama villagers. Ask a player to read out the clues to this village culture, which are printed on every playing board. Then explain how the final scores were calculated.

3.40 Ask leaders to form small groups and to explore the discussion questions with the participants. Give groups time to look at a couple of Bible references, and to do some quiet thinking.

4.00 Close with a time of worship, following the theme of the game.

ESSENTIAL RULES

1 Each team must have 6-8 members. One member should take charge of the score card, noting start and finish times, as well as solution chosen and voting pattern for each problem.

2 When the signal to start is given, a member of your team should pick up the first of the problem cards, read it aloud, and call for a group decision by vote. Players may each register one positive vote for the solution (a, b, c or d) of their choice. They may also each register one dissenting vote for the solution they most dislike. The scorer should record these votes, add them up and record the result. A majority of one is enough to gain a result. A coin may be tossed in case of a deadlock. Note that players may create their own solution (option d) if desired.

3 As soon as a decision is reached, the token may be moved two spaces forward from the Start position. The score card could be completed as the next card is selected. Bonus points are given to teams that finish early.

4 The process is repeated with every card. When your token reaches the finish, stand as a team and signal noisily to the organiser that you have finished.

SAMPLES

Playing board

The board has 25 squares, the first labelled 'Start', and the last labelled 'Finish'. A sketch of some mud huts decorates the centre of the board, and the rest of the space is taken up with a copy of the 'Essential Rules', a pile of problem cards and some Background Information. This information runs as follows.

BACKGROUND INFORMATION
- Your group is a powerful Australian foreign aid body, with excellent contacts in high political circles. You have authority to override the Boama village council if they resist you.
- The Boama village council meets weekly to discuss local problems. It tends to be slow in its decision-making because village harmony is greatly prized and all 107 villagers attend the meeting.
- The Boama villagers live in backward Shishkebab province, and are citizens of Lower Backistan. Despite their low cash income, they enjoy their own mud-brick homes, cattle herds, gardens, and communal lifestyle.
- The neat church building reflects the sincere Christian faith of the villagers. The only grumble they have concerns water. When their rainwater tanks run empty during the long dry season, they face a 12 km return trip to the nearby lake.

LEARNING ON THE RUN

PROBLEM No.	SOLUTION CHOSEN (IF 'D', WRITE IT HERE ↓)	VOTING RECORD			JUDGES' USE ONLY
		SOLUTION	FOR	AGAINST	
ONE	We want a windmill! ↙	A	1	2	
		B	2	5	
		C	0	1	decision made! (+2)
		(D)	5	0	
TWO		A	3	2	dissent
		(B)	4	3	(+2) (-30)
		C	1	2	
		D	0	1	
THREE		(A)	8	0	← (+50) (+2)
		B	0	4	Unanimous
		C	0	2	
		D	0	2	
FOUR		(A)	8	0	← (+50) (+2)
		B	0	6	
		C	0	1	
		D	0	1	
FIVE		(A)	8	0	(Unanimous +50)
		B	0	5	← (+2)
		C	0	3	
		D	0	0	
SIX	Take legal action against multinational company! ↙	A	0	4	
		B	0	0	
		C	0	4	(+2) +3
		(D)	8	0	← +50 (third to finish)

(USE REVERSE SIDE FOR PROBLEMS 7-12) ↓

Note that the Judges' secret scoring system is as follows:
- Each decision made = 2 points (Maximum 24)
- Bonus for early finishing is: 1st = 10 points, 2nd = 6, 3rd = 3.
- Each decision reached unanimously = 50 points.
- If a decision has some votes placed 'against' it, deduct 10 points for each dissenting vote. (Thus a decision made on the basis of a '5 for '2 against' vote would lose 20 points.)
- If a specially created solution (using the 'd' option) mentions the process of consulting the villagers, award 5 points.

Score card
An example is shown at left

Problem cards
These are shown overleaf

BOARD GAMES

1 Your field observer has noted the inefficiency of the 12 km return journey to get water. For up to 9 months of the year, women walk the distance, carrying large clay jars. Suggested solutions are:
(a) Drill a bore, install a large diesel pump to meet drinking water needs and introduce an irrigation scheme.
(b) Provide a robust 6-wheel-drive truck to transport the women.
(c) Provide hand tools for the digging of a traditional well, paying the workers with grain and cattle.
(d) None of the above. Write your own solution.

2 The village has suffered many bitter disputes ever since the new well was created. Your field observer has noted that these disputes used to be discussed and resolved by the women on their long walks to get water. Some women wish that the well had never been dug. The suggested solutions are:
(a) Close the well until the complaints dry up.
(b) Charge villagers a small fee if they choose to use the well.
(c) Bring in a psychologist (with legal training) to resolve disputes.
(d) None of the above. Write your own.

3 The well has suffered serious pollution because of the mess village cattle create when being watered. Even boiling does little to restore the purity of the water. The observer suggests:
(a) Shoot the most offensive animals.
(b) Make livestock drink at the lake, 6 km away.
(c) Charge a substantial fee for herd-watering rights, and spend the money on a new well for human use only.
(d) None of the above. Write your own.

4 The well has suffered serious pollution because of the mess villagers create when laundering clothes, cleaning cook pots, etc. The observer requests urgent action, suggesting:
(a) Shoot the most offensive villagers.
(b) Make housewives rinse nappies at a lake at least 6 km away.
(c) Close the well until villagers treat it with respect.
(d) None of the above. Write your own.

5 A substantial number of the villagers' beloved cattle have been stolen, and the locals are almost certain that the detested Mbulu tribe are the culprits. Your observer reports that the best solutions are:
(a) Sell the theft-prone cattle, and graze wool-producing merinos instead.
(b) Launch a punitive strike, burning down a few Mbulu huts.
(c) Ask the National Army to station soldiers in the village, first requesting that the 'free-loving' troopers have an AIDS test.
(d) None of the above. Write your own.

6 The villagers sold off all their old-style grain to buy the latest high-tech, high-yield hybrid seed from a Western multinational company. The crop was huge, but experiments have revealed that the harvest grain is sterile, and can only be used as food. Your observer suggests:
(a) Sell some of the harvest to buy more exotic hybrid seed.
(b) Sell some of the harvest to buy low-yield traditional seed.
(c) Adopt a cautious 'wait-and-see' approach, doing more tests.
(d) None of the above. Write your own.

7 A prosperous foreign-owned tourist network has offered the village a deal. If villagers agree to pose semi-naked in traditional clothing for tourists, and to allow a 'whites-only' bar to be constructed, the reward will be a school and a clinic. Suggestions are:
(a) Accept the deal, because the school and clinic are needed.
(b) Compromise, accepting the school in return for the bar.
(c) Compromise, accepting the clinic in return for photo posing.
(d) None of the above. Write your own.

8 Massive sheet erosion will ruin the valley unless the current over-grazing is brought under control. The observer suggests:
(a) Reduce all herds by 66 per cent within one month.
(b) Stock no cattle (except some milking cows) for five years.
(c) Keep the three best herds, and force other owners to sell.
(d) None of the above. Write your own.

9 Civil war brings hundreds of refugees through the village every week, most of whom stay for 24 hours. Arriving desperately thirsty, they use huge amounts of water. The well was not designed to cope with such numbers, and there are fears that it might dry up. Your field observer suggests:
(a) To save the well, direct all outsiders to the nearby lake.
(b) Give refugees all the water they want, even if the well fails.
(c) Ration water to refugees, allowing a 24 hour stay only.
(d) None of the above. Write your own.

10 A forest of Australian blue gums was planted ten years ago to provide firewood for the villagers' traditional stoves. The gums are much larger and faster growing than the local trees, which is an advantage for fuel and shade purposes. Unfortunately, they are drying up the supply of underground water rapidly, and the well has had to be deepened several times. Your observer suggests:
(a) Remove all gums immediately and introduce kerosene stoves.
(b) Replace gums slowly with local trees over the next 60 years.
(c) Dig the well deeper each year and ration water.
(d) None of the above. Write your own.

11 The Unpopular Liberation Front is now active in the area and boasts that it will overthrow the corrupt national government within the next five years. Ruthless and heavily armed, they have told the village to show support or suffer the consequences. The field observer suggests:
(a) Pretend to be loyal to both the government and the Front.
(b) Demand regular air patrols by government helicopter gunships.
(c) Encourage your young men to support the liberation movement.
(d) None of the above. Write your own.

12 The Unpopular Liberation Front has come to power, bringing the whole country superb living standards. Every family now has a modern home, car and savings. The villagers learn that Australia has suffered greatly in the aftermath of World War Three, and is in need of urgent help. Your observer suggests that Australia requests one of the following:
(a) A shipment of unwanted corn meal.
(b) A plane-load of economic advisers from Lower Backistan.
(c) Large loans at a nominal 19 per cent interest rate.
(d) None of the above. Write your own.

Discussion questions

- Read through Jesus' prayer for his followers in John 17:6-25, noting especially verses 20-23.
- Why did Jesus put so much emphasis on unity?
- Unity in decision making is obvious in Acts 6:1-7, 13:1-4, 15:22,28. Should a group of Christians make decisions by using formal meeting procedures?
- What reasons can you give for the popu-larity of voting on a motion, compared with seeking consensus?
- What are the strengths and weaknesses of the consensus method?
- Does it matter if a church decision leaves 1 per cent of the congregation angry and upset? See 1 Corinthians 12.
- How important is it to consult with people, rather than imposing ideas on them?
- How different would this game have been if your group had operated by consensus for every problem card?
- Why would consensus decision-making be important for the people of Boama village?

VARIATIONS

1 To make the game more challenging, do not list possible solutions on the problem cards - ask players to think of their own. Note that this will slow the game somewhat, and make it harder for the judges to assess scores.

5. Youth camp

18 - 40   1 - 1.5 hours   8 - 80

DESCRIPTION

This game can be used for training, for detecting ability or for awareness-building. Players work their way through a variety of problem cards, which help them to see youth camping from a new angle. The game could be helpful for parents, new leaders, directors of camps, and administrators, all of whom will learn, or be reminded of, some basic and valuable lessons. It soon reveals how much experience of camping a leader has; and it has often led to the detection of potential new camps directors.

The game's format appears to be competitive; players tackle problems in turn, vote, and tokens creep around the board towards the finishing line. But in fact, as players struggle with the problem cards, they will gain a real sense of being partners in the strategic ministry of Christian camping. The game usually ends with a panel of experts attempting to solve some of the more controversial problems, and to answer questions from the audience.

CHECKLIST

- Playing board, tokens, problem cards and rules for each group (see Samples).
- Written copies of problems for panel members.

PREPARATION

1 Read through the sample questions. Delete, add, render more complex, etc, until they are of a suitable standard for your group.

2 Discuss your final list with any co-leaders, and make any final changes.

3 Prepare sets of problem cards, playing boards (with about 30 squares on each), tokens for each players, and any other necessary resources. Ensure that your guest panel receive copies of the problems in time to study them.

4 Check that the playing area is large enough. Players could sit at tables or on the floor. Remember that you will need to address the whole group at the beginning and end of the game.

5 If you plan to consolidate the learning experience by selling books, ensure that the bookstall team have time to order some quality stock.

RUNNING THE ACTIVITY

This is how the game might run at a training conference for young leaders.

2.00 Gather your co-leaders and panel for a final briefing. Set up the playing area, placing problem cards face-down on the boards.

2.30 Welcome the players, explain the game and its rules and deal with any questions. Form playing groups and let the game begin.

2.45 Along with any helpers, move about quietly, ensuring that groups play at a steady pace and obey the rules.

3.15 Check to see if groups have had enough. If so, close the game and ask players to be ready to refer controversial questions to the panel.

3.30 If discussion has run its course, thank the panel, mention the bookstall, and give players some free time over a tea break.

ESSENTIAL RULES

1 Each playing group has 4-8 members, all of whom select a token and place it on the 'start' square. One or more players should offer to act as time-keeper.

2 When asked to begin, the player with the biggest feet is to select a card from the pile, and has 60 seconds to read the problem out aloud and to come up with a solution. The group is to listen in silence while this happens. When time is up, the timekeeper is to call for a vote, and slam his right hand down on the floor (or table-top).

3 To vote, players place their right hands on top of the timekeeper's. An open hand is a vote of approval for the answer just given. A fist is a vote against. The timekeeper keeps score, and the player's token moves forward (or back) the necessary number of spaces.

5 Debates are not to be entered into. Any controversial matters should be noted and saved for the panel discussion at the end of the game.

SAMPLES

Problem cards

These 'problems' are a mixed bag, relating to the needs of parents, campers, leaders and camps directors. You may need to be quite selective in picking out examples which will meet your needs.

1 An epileptic camper at your adventure camp wishes to participate in all the activities. She is a fit and enthusiastic 16 year old. A nurse on your team, however, feels strongly that it is too risky for an epileptic to be allowed to participate in the horse-riding or in the canoeing. As the camp's director, your decision is?

2 Your two well-meaning voluntary cooks are trying hard to stay within their budget. The campers complain of being underfed, and some of the leaders agree. As director, what do you do?

3 You strongly suspect that a senior camper has been smoking 'pot' at camp, and now a Christian camper tells you that the same person is offering the drug to others. The Christian camper wants to ring the police immediately. As director, your response is?

4 You are a cabin-group leader, and have a big problem. One of your campers is clumsy, lazy and speaks little English. The other cabin members either ignore her, or make sarcastic remarks. Some are even prepared to throw her and her gear out of the cabin. What can you do?

5 At a junior co-ed camp, your cabin group has just been caught 'with their pants down' when another cabin-group (of the oposite sex) peeps over the shower block wall. Your kids are embarrassed and upset. What do you do?

6 You are the pastor of the church, and have just driven to the parish summer camp at a forest campsite. As you drove, you saw smoke in the sky, and Fire Authority trucks on the road. At camp, no one has heard or noticed anything. You try the phone, but all the lines seem jammed. The final evangelistic service has about 30 minutes to go, and will be followed by a celebration dinner. What do you do?

7 Some of your money has definitely disappeared from your luggage, and only two campers have been in the cabin without you being present. You suspect one child in particular, because he is very poorly dressed. How do you handle it?

8 You are the parent of a shy 10-year-old who is going on her first camp. She doesn't know anyone else on the station platform. The leaders, ignoring the kids, spend all their time exchanging personal news, and the train is not due for 15 minutes. What should you do?

9 You are a 15-year-old, attending your first camp. You don't know anyone, but all the others seem to have come in groups. Your tentmates have not even spoken to you yet, and camp started four hours ago. The dinner bell has just rung. How would you cope?

10 You are director of the camp and pride your self on your 'firm and fair' discipline. A young teenage camper from a broken home has so far stolen money, broken windows, attacked three smaller campers and refused duties. Although the team has made every effort to show love and acceptance, he has just told you to 'Go forth and multiply' in front of the whole camp. Your response is?

11 Your co-leader in the cabin is meant to share all responsibilities with you, but seems to just stare into space during studies and games. You feel exhausted, bitter and angry. What should you do?

BOARD GAMES

12 You are a parent of a 10-year-old boy, attending his first camp. He has just phoned you, after being at camp for 24 hours. He is desperately homesick, and sobs endlessly. The camp cost $150, and is meant to run for six days. What do you do?

13 A particularly silly teenage girl is in your small hiking group. About 8 km out of camp, she yells that a snake has bitten her on the leg. Nobody else saw any snake, and no bite is visible among all the scratches on her leg. How do you handle the situation?

14 During the daily meeting one leader objects to the high noise levels and sloppy manners at mealtimes. Other leaders shout her down as being too 'middle class.' As director, how should you handle this?

15 As a raw new tent-leader, you are simply not coping. The kids are rude, uncooperative and bored. What should you do?

VARIATIONS

1 It is sometimes worth grading the cards, so that players initially tackle easy ones, and progress steadily to more demanding ones. You can set this up by relating a different set of cards to each side of the playing board. Set (a) is for the first 7-8 squares, set (b) for the next, etc.

2 It might be helpful to allow players to work in pairs, with veterans assisting novices.

LAWS OF CHRISTIAN EDUCATION III

Seventh law of Christian education
'Total recall is linked to total involvement.'

A lecture on camping skills is not a match for a week away under canvas. People remember best if immersed in the learning process. Give participants the chance to use all their senses, and to involve emotions, intellect and imagination. The *intensity* and the *duration* of the learning activity are key factors. If you really need to drive a point home, be generous with both. Try a simulation or wide-game.

Ninth law of Christian education
'The learning wheel must run the full circle.'

'Praxis' is the original Greek name for the book of Acts in the Bible. These days it is used to describe a learning cycle of 'doing' and 'reflecting'. There is something very healthy about trying your hand at an activity, and then being able to step back and analyse your progress. Jesus used this method to train his disciples. The idea is to keep the wheel turning, giving learners constant exposure to action/reflection/action and so on.

Eighth law of Christian education
'Inside every ugly toad lies a handsome prince.'

Look for the concealed teaching points in every apparent 'disaster' that strikes while you are teaching. An explosion of temper by a participant might lead to a lesson on anger and forgiveness. Be flexible enough to change course, if only temporarily, in order to learn from an unexpected situation. When you respond in this way, you are demonstrating your concern for the needs of the group members. There are no prizes for pig-headed rigidity in Christian education.

Chapter seven

Values clarification activities

What exactly are they?

In popular usage, the term 'values clarification' applies to any activity which helps people explore their values and beliefs. Participants clarify what they believe and discover how important these beliefs are to them. For example, Samantha might discover that her standards of honesty are inconsistent - that she expects high standards of others, but is lax herself. Cecil may be surprised to learn that his 'modern' personal code of ethics is similar to one jotted down by Moses over 3,000 years ago.

To be more precise, the process of 'clarifying' is just one of many ways of exploring values and beliefs. The activities in this chapter could also be used to 'compare', 'contrast', 'evaluate', 'assess', 'empathise', or to 'study conflicts'.

Don't they destroy people's faith

A powerful tool can be used to create things, or to destroy them. The activities in this chapter are powerful tools, and should be treated with respect; I have, therefore, set out clear guidelines below. Properly used, these activities have enormous potential for evangelism and discipleship training.

Is there a risk in using these activities?

The risk arises in those values activities which only stress the different pooints of view on a given topic. If participants do nothing but look at a bewildering array of different moral values, they can become converts to relativism, a belief that there are no absolute truths. For example, an activity might prove that it is morally correct for a Frenchman to have only one wife, and equally correct for a Saudi Arabian to have several. The conclusion could then be (wrongly) drawn that 'there are no fixed moral standards'. A more thoughtful approach would explore the arguments for monogamy and polygamy, and note that the Bible could be quoted to support either. You would need to cover the relevant bibical teaching on marriage, sexuality and relationships; and stress the importance of socio-economic and cultural factors. The outcome would not be relativism, but a deeper understanding of the Christian ideal of marriage.

Can values be rated as good or bad?

Some academics, such as Lawrence Kohlberg, believe that there is a 'development' pattern in human moral thinking. He argues that children initially judge 'right and wrong' according to the certainty of punishment or rewared. They later learn to treat some others as they would like to be treated themselves. Next comes more awareness of the feeling of others, and a desire to conform. A broader awareness of others comes next, followed by a new stage which challenges the rights of the majority to trample the minority. Finally comes a desire to put 'truth' and 'love' before the demands of the State. It can be argued that Christians should seek to progress according to this model. For example, Hubert's driving style should not be determined solely by the presence or absence of a police car (this would be 'primitive' moral thinking). As a

Christian, Hubert should want to respect road laws, road safety, and the needs of others; he might ultimately need to park illegally to save a life. (That is sophisticated moral thinking, involving a decision on moral priorities.)

How can people make moral progress?

Humans are complicated; we do not move permanently forward in neat stages. A threat to our safety might see us drop back from sophistication to 'the law of the jungle'. People can, however, be encouraged to make progress in their moral thinking. Appropriate strategies can help people to 'put themselves in another person's shoes', and thus to realise that certain actions cause others to suffer. Others might need to learn that moral choices are not always black and white; for example, it may seem necessary to kill a crazed gunman before he murders a busload of children. According to one academic, Jack Fraenkel, some of the most useful 'strategies' for encouraging moral progress are:

- Clarifying personal beliefs (and noticing the beliefs of others).
- Comparing and contrasting values, noting different points of view.
- Developing the ability to empathise, understanding how others feel.
- Exploring conflicts between values (e.g. fighting for peace).
- Learning how to evaluate a proposal, and to assess likely consequences.

This chapter provides activities which implement such strategies.

Choosing the tools to make it happen

If you know the sort of moral development your group needs, and if you have identified the appropriate strategy to encourage change, you next need to select a tool to put the strategy into effect. For example you may want to make your group aware of how other cultures view a particular moral issue. The most useful strategy will be to compare and contrast values; an appropriate tool for this job might be an Oxford Debate or a Reaction Game. You will soon see how the activities in this chapter could be used.

Resources

Try these academic textbooks for detailed information;
- Fraenkel, J R *Helping students think and value*, Prentice-Hall, 1980.
- Kirschenbaum/Simon, *Readings in values clarification*, Winston Press, 1973.
- Macquarie, J (Ed.) *A dictionary of Christian Ethics*, SCM, 1984.
- Munsey, B (Ed.), *Moral development, moral education, and Kohlberg*, Religious Education Press, 1980.

1. Reaction game: Think for yourself

10 - 100   0.5 - 1 hr   10 - 1000

DESCRIPTION

Reaction games are from the family of 'forced-choice' exercises. Players are forced to respond to statements by making choices expressed in this case by walking to one side or the other of the playing area. Players thus publicly *declare* their response. To do this, they have to *clarify* their own thinking. They are also made aware of the beliefs of other players, and are later able to *compare* and *contrast* personal beliefs.

Not only does this game help players perform the values tasks mentioned above (clarify, declare, compare, contrast); it also helps the leader of a group to understand where members stand on significant issues, and to discover their level of Christian commitment or openness to the gospel. Teaching programs can then be adjusted accordingly.

This game is often used on the first day of a conference or camp. Players typically find it to be amusing, mentally demanding and a great icebreaker. They are left with lots of hot topics to discuss, and tend to feel more relaxed about sharing their beliefs. The game could lead straight into a formal teaching time, or discussion in small groups.

You can easily raise or lower the standard of the game to suit the ability of your group. It is just as effective with university graduates as it is with semi-literate teenagers.

CHECKLIST

- Copies of the statements for the announcer and for discussion leaders (see Samples).
- Copies of discussion questions for leaders (see Samples).
- A Bible for each participant.

PREPARATION

1 You will need a playing area with enough room for the group to assemble centrally, and then move several steps to the left or right. The announcer must be able to be seen and heard by all players; this will involve a public-address system if the group is large. If the game is to be followed by small group work or some other activity, you will need to arrange appropriate space, furniture and leaders.

2 The list of statements must be appropriate for the needs and abilities of your group, or players will not be able to react to them in a fruitful way. Aim for short and positive statements. They could also be amusing, threatening, challenging, or encouraging. Call in some fellow leaders, test your list on them, adjust as necessary, then draw up a neat version for printing. Copies should be given to the announcer and to any leaders of discussion groups.

3 The game should not be used in isolation. The simplest form of follow-up activity would be small-group discussions, perhaps guided by a leader who has a copy of the statements and of prepared discussion questions. More elaborate activities would be panel discussions, lectures, or written exercises. Whatever your choice, prepare thoroughly.

4 Appoint an announcer who will read out the statements clearly. Allow this person to read through the list in advance, so that nothing is mumbled or fumbled. You may wish to appoint a 'roving reporter' (described below), who has the task of doing short on-the-spot interviews during the game. Both announcer and reporter may need some rehearsal to be most effective, or you could select them on the spot from the ranks of participants so the game looks much less threatening to new players. Leaders can mingle with players and join in the game (subtly encouraging individualism).

RUNNING THE ACTIVITY

This is how the game might run:

1.00 Brief all leaders and assistants for the last time. Check the PA system.
1.30 Welcome players, explain the basic rules, answer any questions and perhaps read out a couple of sample statements. When all is ready, call the announcer to the microphone.
1.40 The game begins when the first statement is read aloud, and players move to their left or right to indicate agreement or disagreement. The reporter strikes, asking one player to explain their choice (in one sentence). The group is called back to the centre, and the next statement is read out. This process continues until 15-20 statements have been read.
2.10 Thank players for their participation, and direct them to the follow-up activity. Form small groups if a discussion is to follow.
2.15 Discussion groups respond to the experience they have just been through, re-visit any particularly interesting statements, and then work through the questions provided.
2.40 Participants unite for closing remarks. It may be appropriate to offer bookstall resources, counselling, or worship.

ESSENTIAL RULES

1 Players must wait silently in the centre of the playing area while the announcer reads a statement.

2 They should then, without comment, move to their left to indicate agreement, or to their right to indicate disagreement.

3 They should remain in this position until any interviews are completed, and until asked to return to the centre by the announcer.

4 This pattern will be repeated until all the statements have been read.

5 Loud debates (over any controversial matters) should be delayed until the game is over and discussion groups are formed.

6 Players must respond as individuals, and not just stay with the herd.

SAMPLES

Statements for the announcer

- all cats should be banned from suburban areas.
- All dogs should be banned from suburban areas.
- McDonald's hamburgers are made of plastic.
- McDonald's hamburgers are made of something far worse than plastic.
- Human inventions have done more harm than good.
- Christian marriage is just an ideal, quite out o touch with real life.
- Science has proved that the Bible cannot be trusted.
- The people listening to this statement are more modest than average.
- People who can't make quick decisions are wishy-washy.
- Jesus remains as one of the most fascinating people in history.
- Everybody has some interest in the topic of life after death.
- The Bible refers largely too real people and places in history.
- People are more important than whales or dolphins.
- Very sick people over the age of 40 should be put to sleep.
- In God's opinion, every human life is precious.
- The life and teachings of Jesus reveal his identity as Son of God.
- It's O.K. for Christians to watch R-rated films.
- It's O.K. for Christians to attend a nudist club.
- Starving people overseas should look after themselves.
- People aged under 21 are too young to marry.
- People aged over 14 should be allowed to drive.
- Staring at a night sky with billions of stars in a religious experience.
- All religions are basically the same.
- It is always best to play it safe, and stay with the herd.
- This game has gone on long enough!

Discussion questions

These are suitable for young Christian adults.
- How did you feel about having to publicly show your responses by moving?
- Should our lifestyle make our beliefs obvious? If so, how?
- Were you surprised to notice that the group disagreed on so many matters?
- Do your friends expect you to conform or to think independently?
- Which was the toughest question for you to respond to? Why?
- When do you get the chance to discuss 'heavy' topics, such as religion?
- Why are most people so shy about discussing religious beliefs?
- Do you now feel more relaxed about expressing your beliefs? Why?
- Does disagreement on an important topic

VALUES CLARIFICATION ACTIVITIES

mean that the majority is right, or that all are wrong?
- How should Christians go about discovering truth when a difficult issue confronts them (e.g. The question of killing very sick people aged over 40)?
- How do your feel when your friends disagree strongly with you on a topic?
- How should the Church cope with disagreement on important topics?
- Explore these verses to see what the Bible says about finding truth: II Timothy 3:10-17, Luke 1:1-4, Acts 15:6-21,28. Note how the Acts verses mention prayerful discussion, Scripture and experience. Truth is usually not arrived at until all three of these elements are in harmony.

VARIATIONS

1 You could ask players to indicate more subtle degrees of response to the statements. Instead of simply demonstrating full agreeement or disagreement, they could stay in a central spot (to register 'no decision'), or move as far to the left or right as they choose (to indicate degrees of response).

2 The group could record their responses on paper while seated at tables. This allows privacy, but at the expense of the healthy group dynamics of the method outlined above. A simple linear graph (see below) could be printed for each statement, with participants placing an 'X' to record their responses.

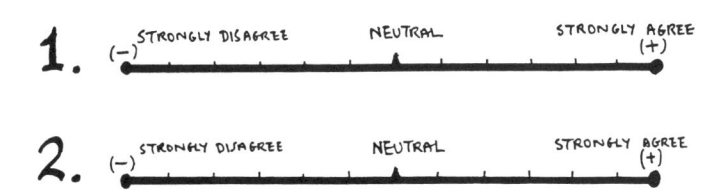

1. STRONGLY DISAGREE (−) ———— NEUTRAL ———— STRONGLY AGREE (+)

2. STRONGLY DISAGREE (−) ———— NEUTRAL ———— STRONGLY AGREE (+)

2. Oxford debate: The starting point

16 - 100   1 - 1.5 hours   12 - 1000

DESCRIPTION

The term 'Oxford Debate' relates to the old university custom of involving audiences in debating competitions. This version has four debating 'teams', each with a different argument to present. They make short statements in rapid succession, so the pace stays hot. The audience stands centrally, and indicates agreement or disagreement with the speakers by walking towards convincing speakers, and away from the others. The audience mills around in splendid confusion. Speakers may challenge members of the audience, demanding a reason for their change of position. (This guarantees that the audience is kept on the alert!) It is the perfect way to look at the spread of opinion on a controversial issue.

This debate is called 'The Starting Point' because it takes as a starting point four different belief systems. As the debate progresses, the arguments develop in a logical manner. Players will be forced to do some hard thinking about their personal beliefs, and the scene is set for some lively discussions and teaching. It is suitable for both discipleship training and evangelism. The lesson is that our beliefs are very important. We need to know what our declared values are based on, and we need to build a lifestyle that is in true harmony with them.

CHECKLIST

- Copies of the script for speakers and discussion leaders (see Samples).
- Copies of discussion questions for leaders (see Samples).
- A Bible for each participant.

PREPARATION

1 You will need a playing area large enough for the audience to stand centrally, then move to and fro with the four speakers standing on tables in each of the corners. You may need to arrange for a public-address system if the audience is large. The post-game discussion and teaching time will require adequate space and furniture.

2 Your most difficult task is the creation of a script for the various speakers. You need to relate it to the spiritual and intellectual needs of the audience. See Samples on page 125 and 126 for ideas on how to set it out. Keep statements short, positive, and clear. Ask your co-leaders to check it before printing copies. You may also wish to print some discussion questions and other follow-up material.

3 Select and brief people for the following roles, and give them copies of the script.

- Discussion leaders. They need copies of the script and the discussion questions.
- A 'Roving Reporter' to interview players during the game. After players have moved in response to a statement, the reporter should pounce on a victim, quickly ask why they moved, and seek a brief response. The reporter must not comment on the answers and should allow shy players to decline being interviewed. Controversial answers can be handled in the discussion time later.
- Four speakers. It may be wise to give the roles to group members, and to allow your leaders to participate as part of the audience. This prevents any 'them and us' feelings, and means that some players will be more willing to reveal their beliefs.

VALUES CLARIFICATION ACTIVITIES

If speakers are to wear costumes, explain what is needed.

4 The debate should not be held in isolation. The audience will want to discuss matters raised by the speakers, and will probably have plenty of questions. The ideal follow-up is small group discussion, followed by a 'forum' where players can present their questions or statements. You may need to ensure that Bibles are available for everybody.

RUNNING THE ACTIVITY

This is how the debate might run:

2.00 Brief the four speakers and reporter for the last time. Check the PA system, and any supplies of printed material.

2.30 As Chairperson, welcome players, explain the rules and answer any questions. The four speakers might read out a sample statement each. When all is ready, ask the first speaker to begin.

2.40 The first speaker makes a statement, following the script. You then invite players to respond by moving closer to the speaker (indicating agreement), or further away (to indicate disagreement). Now is the time for a roving reporter to appear and choose a 'victim'.

2.45 The second speaker now makes a statement, following the script. The above process is repeated. The same applies for the third and fourth speakers. The first 'round' is now over.

2.55 The second 'round' of statements could involve a change of speaking order. Otherwise the ingredients are the same.

3.05 The third round might be faster-paced. All four speakers read their statements in rapid succession, there is a pause for audience movement, then the statements are read again. As soon as movement settles, the reporter pounces on two or three victims. This approach forces the players to concentrate more carefully. If players cannot cope, revert to the initial pattern. If all is well, continue with the fast-paced version.

3.15 The remaining rounds take place, and the audience begins to stabilise in its position as players clarify their thinking.

3.30 Announce the end of the debate, thanking participants, speakers and the reporter. Move everybody into discussion groups, asking them to write down any difficult questions for the forum to deal with.

3.50 Call the group back together and invite players to toss questions at an expert panel.

The panel members could liven things up by involving the audience in the answering process; they could also deliberately argue amongst themselves, or make provocative statements. However because this is the final phase of the activity, beware of stirring up divisions in the audience. The mood should be one of intellectual stimulation and of emotional stability.

4.00 Close the activity, but be aware of the needs of players. Some may need counselling, or some helpful reading material; others may be shocked at the discovery that so much disagreement exists in the group. You could provide a long coffee-break, or a furious game of volleyball.

ESSENTIAL RULES

1 Players must remain still (and silent) in the central playing area while the speakers are talking. When asked by the chairperson to respond, players should move towards a speaker to show agreement and away to show disagreement.

2 If a roving reporter asks a player to explain their choice of position, the player may decline, but otherwise will give a short one-sentence reply. No further discussion is called for.

3 Long and complex arguments are welcome - but only during the discussion *after* the debate.

4 Players must respond as individuals rather than staying with the herd.

SAMPLES

Speakers

These are the world views of the four speakers:

A Conservative Christian: believable, but demonstrates right-wing political bias and a very literal approach to Scripture.

B Radical Christian: believable, but demonstrates left-wing political bias and a more daring way of interpreting the Bible.

C Humanist: shows concern for humanity, but drifts into a mixture of 'hippy think', New Age ideas and selfish individualism.

D Rationalist: thinking is hard, logical and shaped by Darwin's evolutionary model and Scientific Socialism.

In each of the rounds, the speakers (A, B, C, D) present their lines to the audience as requested by the chairperson. The order of presentation may vary in each round.

Script

Round one - The starting point'

A An all-powerful God made the earth in six, 24-hour days in 4,004 BC.

B God made the world millions of years ago. Genesis tells us *why*, science tells us *how*.
C The planets aligned perfectly, allowing a huge gas cloud to condense and form the earth. All this happened billions of years ago.
D Earth is an accident, formed by a random big-bang exactly 4,500 million years ago.

Round two - 'The status of humans'
A Man was made in God's image, and designed to love and fear him.
B Humans have a God-given drive for truth, justice, beauty and happiness.
C Human beings are the top animal, with the possible exception of dolphins and whales.
D Homo-sapiens are accidents, a mutated form of ape, created by chance in Africa around 100,000 BC.

Round three - 'Humans and the enviroment'
A Man was told to fill the earth and subdue it; that means farms, dams, and big families.
B Humans were meant to care for Eden, not to bulldoze it. It was a garden, not a factory.
C Forests have a right to exist. Wilderness, plants and animals have priority over cities.
D The environment is a battleground of strong over weak. Man is the strongest animal and can control or destroy the natural forces.

Round four - 'The purpose of life'
A Living in peace with God, obeying his laws, comes before King, country, and politics.
B We should live as radical disciples, opposing the evils of oppressive governments and greedy multi-nationals.
C Human freedom is a right. We each do what seems good for us at the time.
D What really matters is the quest for power, which is the driving force behind all humans.

Round five - 'What is truth?'
A God is truth. Truth can be found in God's character, revelation, word and creation.
B Truth is gained when Christian people draw on Scripture, apply it to life and prayerfully discuss the results.
C Truth is linked to the 'greatest good for the greatest number'.
D Truth lies in the scientific study of the life-struggle throughout the cosmos. Truth lies with the winners, not with the losers.

Round six - 'Laws, morals and ethics'
A The Bible shows us it is black and white. We have the ten commandments. There are no 'grey areas' for the true believer.
B The Bible is full of ideals, but allows for compromise in a fallen world (e.g. regulations for divorce, slavery, use of armies).
C It all comes down to individual choice. For example, the terminally ill and aged should be able to request a life-terminating injection.
D Why have laws which burden the strong? Painless and clinical solutions are available to neutralise the problem members of our community.

Round seven - 'The future'
A In a sinful, fallen world Christians should hang on faithfully until the second coming of Christ.
B Christians should actively continue the fight for a world free of slavery, war, injustice and pollution.
C The human animal is constantly evolving, making continuous progress towards perfection.
D Brave new leaders are needed to lead humanity to glory. Where are the Stalins, Hitlers and Pol-Pots to create a perfect new Master-Race?

Discussion questions

- How consistent were the speakers? Did their arguments develop in a logical way from the beginning to end?
- Why are foundations so important for a tall building? Why are the foundations for moral beliefs equally important? Would it be possible to believe in a set of 'Ten Commandments' if you also believed that the world was made by chance?
- Did the movements of some players during the game show that they liked the starting point of one speaker, but not that speaker's conclusion?
- Do you have friends who are happy to borrow Christian moral teaching, but prefer to think that the human race is master of the universe?
- Read through the first three chapters of Genesis, noting verses which help you build a theology of creation, conservation and human dignity.
- What differences did you notice between the arguments of the two Christian speakers? (If unsure, ask for a copy of the script.)
- How should Christians cope when they find that they disagree?
- What do Christians have to offer in a world of confused values?

VARIATIONS

1 The questions to the players could be handled by the chairperson or the speakers instead of a Roving Reporter.

2 To make the event more memorable,

encourage the speakers to dress according to the lifestyle and values of their philosophy, e.g. a militaristic scientist, a hippy, a pastor in denims, and another pastor in a neat black suit.

3 You may wish to re-structure the debate, presenting only two points of view. Some veterans assure me that it works best with three rival speakers. It becomes too confusing with more than six speakers.

4 If the speakers do not dress according to Variation 2 (above), why not ask your guests on the discussion panel to do some acting? They could dress as spokespersons of four fictitious societies, and be introduced accordingly. Each could represent one of the four points of view. Note, however, that it is unwise to generate emotional heat during this closing phase of the program.

5 With careful selection of topics and questions, an Oxford debate can be created to meet the needs of children as young as ten.

3. Moral dilemma: The hiding place

DESCRIPTION

'Moral dilemma' activities, if done well, enable participants to identify with the emotions and ethical confusion of the central character in a story of a difficult moral position. The ability to 'walk in someone else's shoes' is a key part of moral development; from it comes improved tolerance and the discovery that moral choices are often not clear-cut.

These activities also focus on a conflict of values. For example, a father may face the choice of stealing a vital drug or letting his child die. The conflict here is between the 'honesty' ethic and the 'value of human life/duty of parent' ethics; it is solved by a process of 'evaluating and assessing,' - a third area of values study. The importance of the conflicting values must be carefully weighed up, and priority given to one of them. This may sound very complex but our brains attempt this operation every time we open a newspaper. There are always stories of people being praised (or blamed) for making difficult moral decisions.

I have drawn the moral dilemma stories in this activity from the autobiography of Corrie ten Boom, *The hiding place*. The main characters are Dutch Christians who paid dearly for their faithful discipleship. As participants learn to empathise, to identify the moral conflicts and to evaluate, they will be challenged to look hard at their own lives. The stories, and the following discussion material, confront people with the challenge of real discipleship. They will also help participants to build a personal ethical system that is truly Christian. Even though the activity is mainly designed to 'stretch' comfortable Christians, it can also be used for evangelism.

CHECKLIST

- Copies of the dilemma stories for group leaders (or each participant) see Samples).
- Copies of discussion questions for group leaders (see Samples).
- Bible, pen and paper for each participant.
- Video or film equipment, if needed.

PREPARATION

1 Arrange a suitable area for discussion groups to operate. The activity requires concentration, so find a place where noise levels witll be low and distractions kept to a minimum. If you plan to conclude with a film or video, check that the equipment is ready to go.

2 Read through the dilemma stories, adapting them if necessary to suit the needs of your group. The stories must be easy to understand, with enough detail for readers to identify with the main characters. Ensure that the difficult choice in the story comes across as difficult for the reader. You need to be aware of the culture, morals and educational standards of your group. The discussion groups will need questions which help them to empathise, identify values conflicts and to resolve by assessing and evaluating. (These processes are explained above in the Description). Meet with your co-leaders, go through the stories and questions with them, make any necessary alterations and print copies for each participant.

3 If your co-leaders have little experience with this type of learning activity, why not do one of the dilemma stories together? You may

VALUES CLARIFICATION ACTIVITIES

wish to call in a local Christian who has some experience or training in this field, and work through all of the stories and questions. See also the following activity in this chapter, which deals with the measurement of values.

4 As this activity is based on a top quality book, why not have copies for sale? The film and video are also superb, so I recommend that you make every effort to hire a copy. See 'Resources'.

5 If your leaders need a clearer understanding of conditions in wartime Holland, watch the video of *The hiding place* together. Other videos or library books might also be useful.

6 Participants should have Bibles, pens and paper.

RUNNING THE ACTIVITY

This is how the activity might proceed.

3.00 Meet with co-leaders for a final briefing and check of equipment. Ensure that all understand the time schedule, because time can fly if groups get into heavy discussions!

3.30 Welcome participants. Set the scene, so that all participants understand what life was like in wartime Holland and are ready to do some hard thinking.

3.40 Form small discussion groups and begin the process of reading through a story, then applying the questions to it. This pattern is repeated for each story.

4.30 Wind up the small group phase with the final set of questions, which will help participants to relate the stories to their own lives.

4.40 All meet together for reports from groups, and any closing remarks. A short worship time could help players focus on the importance of being 'with Christ, or against him'.

5.00 A break for exercise, free-time, drinks, etc., would be appropriate at this stage. The ideal concluding activity would be a screening of the film *The Hiding Place*, and to offer copies for sale. Comic-book versions are available from some Christian bookshops.

RESOURCES

1 The film version of *The Hiding Place*, starring Julie Harris, Eileen Heckart and Arthur O'Connell, was released by World Wide Pictures in the mid 1970's.

2 The paperback *The hiding place*, by Corrie ten Boom with John and Elizabeth Sherrill, was published by Hodder and Stoughton in numerous editions, including one in 1980. It features photos taken from the film.

SAMPLES

Moral dilemma stories

1 You are an elderly grandfather, eighty-four years old. All your life you have worked quietly away in your shop, selling and repairing watches. You feel responsible for your two unmarried daughters, who live with you in rooms above the shop. Over the years you have become a greatly respected Christian leader in your city. To your great sorrow, your country has been invaded and occupied by an evil foreign power which is determined to seek out and destroy all members of a minority racial group. You are committed to non-violence, but decide to defy the evil power and offer protection to members of this persecuted race. Despite threats that any citizen sheltering these people will face brutal punishment, you help many to find safety. You and your family are eventually betrayed, and are being interrogated by the dreaded secret police. You know that you now face torture and execution. To your amazement, the interrogator offers to release you, and send you home! He indicates (out of respect for your age), that he will take your word that you will cause 'no more trouble'. Do you accept this amazing offer, and go home a free man? You have already rescued hundreds of people. Do you defy this powerful official, and go off to certain death? If you annoy the official, will it help your two daughters who are beside you in the room? What is your response?

[Father ten Boom replied calmly that he would always open his door to any person in need who knocked. He was sent to prison, died ten days later and was buried in an unmarked grave. See chapters 10 and 11 in the book.]

2 You work as a watch repairer, and share your home with an elderly father and a sister who is about your age. You are all committed Christians and have gained a reputation for being fanatically honest. At times your honesty has cost you lots of money: you have persuaded customers to have watches repaired rather than buy expensive new ones. Your faith has recently motivated you to get involved in a very dangerous adventure your home is a refuge for members of a persecuted minority race. If you did not help them, they would be arrested and exterminated by the government. You do not have anywhere near enough food to feed them all and food cannot be bought, at any price, unless a ration card is used. A brave and loyal friend mentions that he works in an office which issues ration cards. You realise that he can be trusted completely, and that he will do anything for you. Do you now ask him to steal a large supply of the precious ration cards? If you do, you will be as morally guilty of the theft as he is. What if one (or both) of you is caught and executed? How will you feed the refugees in your house if you don't have ration cards? What is your response? [Corrie ten Boom asked her friend to steal 100 ration cards for her. He did this by arranging for a 'robbery' of his office. To ensure that he was not suspected, he arranged for the robbery to take place during working hours, and asked the 'thief' to beat him severely. The theft was successful. The refugee program was able to continue. See chapter six.]

3 You and your family are all committed Christians. Ever since your country was occupied by an evil foreign power, you have been involved in risky activities, the most dangerous being the provision of food and shelter for a persecuted racial minority. You know that if you were caught by the authorities, you would be tortured and killed. Despite this risk, you have continued to open your door to people in need,. because they would face certain death if you refused to help. Your family feels that they have done everything possible to cope with a raid by the authorities. Within thirty seconds of the police arriving, you could remove all traces of refugees, thanks to warning buzzers and the construction of a secret room. Your greatest fear is that someone will betray you. Now, for the first time, you sense that you are dealing with a double agent. This man insists that he is an ally, but he may be employed as a spy by the authorities,. He begs you to raise some money for him, on the grounds that the money will free his wife from the police station cells. He wants to get her before the dreaded secret police arrive. He assures you that he and his wife have sheltered many refugees. You realise that if the story is true and if you do not help, the woman will be forced to tell the authorities all about her activities. You would then be guilty of betraying a brave fellow rescuer and many lives could be lost. If the man is a traitor, your gift of the money will prove that you are an enemy of the authorities. He implores you to help, but your intuition tells your that he is not to be trusted. On the other hand, you have never refused a request for help before. What is your response? [Corrie ten Boom decided that she could not turn away a person in need and she made arrangements to provide the money. Unfortunately, her intuition had been correct; the man was a traitor. That night her home was raided by the secret police and her whole family was arrested, with some dying at the hands of the authorities. See chapter 9 in the book.]

4 You are proud of your country, and feel deeply angry when an evil foreign power attacks. Despite attempts to stay neutral, your national leaders are left with no option but to attempt resistance. Within five days the invasion is complete, leaving many dead. The enemy is cruel and ruthless. Young men are taken off to forced labour camps, and members of a racial minority group are rounded up for execution. As Christians, you and your family have strong views about justice, non-violence and honesty. Although normally strictly law-abiding, you have all decided to offer shelter to those who are being persecuted. If the authorities discover this, you risk execution. So many refugees have found safety in your home that you have had to steal ration cards from the authorities; otherwise you could not possibly have fed them. In the course of your rescue work comes an unusual request. You are given the name of a dangerous traitor, who has led many to a horrible fate and you are asked to pass his name on to the secret resistance network, who could then execute him. This would be easy to do, because some of those who help you save refugees are also in the resistance movement. You feel confused. Since the invasion you have (for the first time ever) disobeyed the authorities. You have illegally sheltered refugees, stolen huge numbers of ration cards and lied to a policeman about having a radio in the house. Now you must decide whether to pass on this important piece of information. If you pass it on, the alleged traitor will be murdered by the resistance; if you don't, the traitor may cause many of your fellow countrymen to die. What is your response? Corrie ten Boom responded to the request by declaring that she wanted to save life, not destroy it. She prayed for the traitor. She accepted help from members of the armed resistance, but restricted her activities to rescue work. See chapters six and eight in the book.)

Discussion questions

Each story could be explored with these questions.
- How would you feel if you were the person in the story? Describe your likely emotions, and any values and loyalties involved.
- What is your immediate response to the story? How would you act?
- What values appear to be in conflict in this story? List them, and explain why each would be important to the main character.
- Should one of these values have priority over any other? How can this be decided?
- Explore the consequences of each course of action. Does this help you make a clear decision in this case?
- Should the person in the story decide according to conscience or according to the likely consequences?

After all the dilemmas have been tackled, try these questions.

VALUES CLARIFICATION ACTIVITIES

- Should you ever act against your Christian beliefs? What difference does it make if your 'moral purity' puts others at risk?
- Note the boldness of Jesus in facing some tricky moral dilemmas. Read John 8:1-11 and Matthew 12:9-14. What was the effect on the Pharisees, according to Matthew 12:14?
- Should fear influence you in choosing between values? Read Luke 11:23, Luke 12: 8-12, Revelation 3:16, Joshua 24:15-18, Acts 4: 18-20 and Matthew 16:24-27.

VARIATIONS

1 If your group is not very literate, the moral dilemma stories could be read aloud or presented by video or comic-strip.

2 If the World War II setting poses cultural problems, find other stories which feature Christians living under great pressure. Good Christian bookshops stock plenty of books about Christians trying to be faithful in the face of oppression and persecution.

4. Evaluating & assessing: The measuring machine

DESCRIPTION

People in moral dilemmas find that whichever way they turn, they seem to be in danger of breaching long-held values and beliefs. The process of sorting out such problems is known as 'evaluating and assessing' and it requires the slow and careful description of all possible courses of action. Each option is then examined in turn; and finally the options are compared. If all this is done according to a disciplined pattern, the final choice may appear obvious. Failing that, the number of workable options will at least be reduced to a manageable number. Most of us would rather deal with three options than a dozen.

The 'disciplined pattern' mentioned above can be provided by a number of grids (set out in Samples on pages 133 and 134.) This activity shows people how to use the grids. Some imaginary problems are provided for participants to play with. (It would be too threatening to ask them to analyse current personal problems.) As participants become familiar with the process of evaluating and assessing, they will want to do some homework in private. The activity enables them to make carefully measured decisions about very important of spiritual values, the participants learn that the Christian faith applies to every aspect of life. You can emphasise this point by providing problems which are linked closely to the participants' lives. Teenagers will benefit from problems which touch on sexuality, peer-pressure, or school life. Adults will be impressed if you provide problems linked to stress, marriage and finances.

The activity would be useful for both new Christians and mature saints. It would also be enjoyed by many non-Christians. Whether you use it for evangelism of discipleship, the process of sorting out a personal value-system is a stretching and valuable experience.

CHECKLIST

* Bible, pencil and eraser.
* List of problems and discussion questions for each leader (see Samples).
* Worksheets for participants (see Samples).

PREPARATION

1 The participants will appreciate it if you provide chairs and tables for this activity. If that is not possible, ensure that everyone has a chair and a clip-board. You will probably want to be able to address the whole group at the start, and then disperse people into small groups. Check that you will have access to a public address system, overhead projector, and any other equipment that you plan to use.

2 Draw up a list of possible problems for the participants to solve, ensuring that they relate closely to the lifestyle of your group members. (See samples section.) This is vital if the activity is to be seen as relevant. Ask your co-leaders to check this list, and to suggest improvements. Print copies for all group leaders (or all participants).

3 Choose the most appropriate 'grid' to use with the group and either print copies for all, or prepare a wall chart and ask participants to hand copy it. If your group leaders are new to this activity, put them through a full practice run.

4 Participants will need pencils, erasers, paper and Bibles.

VALUES CLARIFICATION ACTIVITIES

RUNNING THE ACTIVITY

This is how the activity might proceed.

1.00 Brief all co-leaders for the last time. Check the PA system and any other equipment to be used.

1.30 Welcome participants and explain the program. Demonstrate how the grids work on a couple of sample dilemmas, using an overhead projector or wall-charts. Explain that small groups will be given a list of problems and that they are allowed ten minutes to put each one on a grid and discuss it.

1.40 Move participants into small groups. Each group should try both individual and team work. It may be wise to move about, ensuring that all groups are coping.

2.20 If groups have had enough, ask them to look up helpful Bible reading values (see Samples).

2.30 Assemble the whole group for a short worship time, then close.

SAMPLES

The positive/negative grid

This is the simplest of the evaluation/assessment grids. The possible action is described at the top. The practical and ethical arguments in favour of the action are listed on the left side of the vertical line and the arguments against it are listed on the right side of the line. With experience, participants may be able to group similar arguments together (e.g. financial, health, family impact); this is helpful because some arguments may tend to cancel each other out. For example, the costs of repairing an ancient car may be similar to the interest payments on a new one. Here is a partially completed grid:

PROPOSED COURSE OF ACTION: *Stamp on police officer's toe*	
'+' ARGUMENTS	**'−' ARGUMENTS**
Become a hero at school	Be arrested
	Family ashamed
	Large fine
	Police file
	Reputation as 'trouble-maker'

This simple process can be very helpful. Setting out problem on paper can banish despair and plant seeds of hope. Note that final decisions should not be based on the sheer number of arguments; it is wise to list all arguments, and then circle the most significant ones. This might reveal, for example, that an otherwise attractive job an offer will do a lot of damage to family life and should be declined.

The short-term/long-term grid

This is similar to the exercise above, but adds the element of time. Participants must attempt to look a few years into the future - not an easy task if they tend to operate one day at a time. In our society, where the media frantically promotes 'instant gratification', Christians should demonstrate a more thoughtful lifestyle. This exercise introduces the important concept of 'delayed gratification'. When discussing this with players, point out that success rarely comes to the 'snoozers', or even the 'sprinters' of this world - it is the determined 'long-distance runners' who achieve their ambitions (e.g. a completed apprenticeship, a house that is paid off, a flourishing youth-group). The book of proverbs is full of home-spun wisdom on this theme.

| PROPOSED COURSE OF ACTION | Abandon nursing course, work in factory |

'+' ARGUMENTS		'−' ARGUMENTS	
SHORT TERM	LONG TERM	SHORT TERM	LONG TERM
More money		Boring work	Lower income
Shorter hours			Boredom
Better social life			Job insecurity
			No promotions

The graded impact grid

This is the 'high-tech' grid for handling anything from routine choices to complex moral dilemmas. First, you write down a proposed course of action, then list and number the possible consequences of this action are listed. Each consequence is then put through the grid, attracting 'positive' or 'negative' scores according to its likely effect on family values, Christian beliefs, health and safety and so on. The person using the grid should decide on the scoring range of each of these factors. For example, if Christian values were prized, the scoring range might be marked as '-50' to '+5'. If the values of friends were of little importance, a range of only '-5' to '+5' might be appropriate. Here is a partially completed grid.

| PROPOSED COURSE OF ACTION | Join French Foreign Legion |

POSSIBLE CONSEQUENCES OF THIS ACTION	Number score
1. Kill a lot of innocent people	−105
2. Moral slide — alcohol, sex	−135
3. Physical injuries	− 35
4. Rise to rank of major in 20-25 years	+ 35
5.	
6.	

SCORING GRID FOR THE ABOVE

CONSEQUENCES

VALUES FACTORS		(1)	(2)	(3)	(4)	(5)	(6)
Faith	+/−50	−50	−50	0	0		
Personal morals	+/−30	−30	−20	0	0		
Family values	+/−25	−20	−25	0	+5		
Legal impact	+/−25	0	0	0	0		
Health	+/−20	0	−20	−20	0		
Friends' values	+/−15	−5	−10	0	+10		
Financial impact	+/−10	0	−10	−10	+10		
Education impact	+/−10	0	0	−5	+10		

VALUES CLARIFICATION ACTIVITIES

With the grid completed, and scores added up, it should be obvious that some of the possible consequences have scored badly. This is a solid clue that the proposed course of action is likely to bring you into conflict with your values. Try to come up with a different course of action and test it on the grid.

If the idea of using number scores does not appeal, try this letter code.

'A' indicates fully acceptable.
'B' means barely acceptable.
'C' is certain to do some damage!
'D' will lead to disaster.

Using this system, a single 'D' score cancels the whole exercise, but two 'C' scores might be tolerated. This has advantages, because our values choices do not always follow a crude 'majority vote wins' pattern.

Note that the left-hand column of 'Values Factors' might need to be varied according to the needs of the user. The values of workmates, organisations, or political causes might need to be added, not to mention aesthetic or environmental preferences. As mentioned above, each player should mark in the scoring power of each factor according to their perception of the moral importance of each one. This exercise alone can be quite demanding for some people.

Problems for evaluation using grids

- As an innocent 16-year-old girl, you want to go for a drive with an oversexed Romeo (aged 21) rather than attend the church youth group.
- You are invited to go shoplifting with some teenage friends.
- At a 21st party, you want to give hallucinogenic drugs a try.
- You are offered a promotion which means many nights away from your children.
- You are dared by your gang to stamp on a police officer's toe.
- Your parents suggest that you abandon your four-year nursing course and take a job in a nearby factory.
- Your best friend wants you to leave your apprenticeship and enlist in the French Foreign Legion. The uniform and travel prospects are attractive.
- You plan to use a bicycle for the next two years until you qualify as an engineer, but a neighbour offers you a luxury car at a bargain price.
- All your friends have taken up hang gliding through caves as a weekend sport. Your husband and four children encourage you to be physically active and money is no problem. Do you join your friends?

Discussion questions

- Read Ephesians, especially from 4:17 to 5:21. What reason does Paul give for his call to a more moral lifestyle? Why should the people at Ephesus be expected to change their ways? What changes does Paul expect?
- Read Philippians 2:1-18. What images and arguments does Paul use in these verses? What qualities are praised most highly?

5. Reflective exercises: Heavy, heavy questions

16 - 100   1 - 1.5 hrs   2 - 1000

DESCRIPTION

Few people make time in their busy lives to sit back and reflect on their values. Sometimes it takes a crisis, such as a long stay in hospital, to force us to evaluate our course through life. When we take time to do this, some stunning discoveries can be made. We may realise that our course through life is controlled by others, or that our life is totally lacking in any sense of direction. We may decide that it is high time to reverse the compass bearing and return to an earlier set of beliefs.

If carried out in a group, the process enables participants to compare and contrast personal values with those of others. Group members first sort out their own life directions. Then they can be asked to join with others and invited to share some of their discoveries. Naturally, this must be done in a supportive and non-threatening small group environment; not many people would want to blurt out personal thoughts to a group of strangers! As individuals make their various contributions, the comparing and contrasting begins. Participants realise that others share their struggles, or that they have chosen to follow bolder paths.

The following samples provide a structure for both personal reflection and group discussion. They can be used with mature Christians, apathetic Christians, and with those enquiring about the faith. The exercises may not look very 'spiritual' initially, but they tend to demolish the usual 'anti-God defences' and leave people open to exploring the claims of the gospel. Older teenagers seem to get as much out of this sort of activity as adults.

CHECKLIST

- Bible, pencil, eraser and note-book for each participant.
- Copies of discussion questions for group leaders (see Samples).
- Exercises for participants (see Samples).

PREPARATION

1 You will need an area where the whole group can meet initially. You also need enough space to scatter the group for some time alone and finally, you need room for participants to gather in small groups. Given suitable weather, the whole exercise could be done outdoors - but avoid areas which will provide distractions.

2 Participants will need printed exercises. If not using the samples provided, draft these with great care and discuss them with your co-leaders. It is essential that the 'reflection exercises' relate closely to the needs and interest of your group. Leaders of small groups will encourage honest, but non-threatening sharing of discoveries and feelings. They may need some training before they feel comfortable about managing this sort of activity. The best preparation would be a trial run.

4 Ensure that you have the resources to follow-up participants after the activity, through both personal visits and helpful literature. Be alert to clues that people are spiritually hungry.

5 Participants will need a note-book, pencil and Bible.

LEARNING ON THE RUN

RUNNING THE ACTIVITY

This is how the activity might proceed.

1.00 Brief all co-leaders for the last time. Check that resources are ready and that furniture is arranged.
1.30 Welcome participants and issue them with exercises. Give a full explanation of the activity, stressing that full privacy may be maintained and that contributions to group discussion will be on a voluntary basis. Allow time for questions.
1.40 Dismiss the group for an agreed period. If necessary, allocate specific areas for each person to use. Wander about from time to time, so that anyone having difficulties with the exercises can consult with you.
2.20 Call participants back together and divide them into small groups, each with a trained leader. Move about quietly from group to group, in case anyone is having difficulties. Participants may benefit from a discussion of some helpful Bible passages (see sample questions below).
2.35 If desired, call the groups back to the central meeting area and formally end the activity. Provide a long tea-break so that conversations can continue.

SAMPLES

Tombstone exercise

Using the full page, draw a large rectangular tombstone. Imagine that this is the marker for *your* grave. Be as honest and realistic as you can, as you add these details to the stone:
- Full name: Write 'Here lies ...'
- Dates (imagine that you have died five years from now.) Write 'Born ....., Died .....'
- State cause of death and likely location, in about six words.
- State the qualities and actions for which people would fondly remember you. Maximum of 40 words. Write 'Remembered for .....'.
- Indicate the breadth of group who would really miss you. Maximum of 20 words. Write 'Greatly missed by ......'.

Island exile

You have been declared guilty of murder, although you are innocent. There is no hope of appeal. You will spend the next 20 years in a lonely island prison, seeing very few other people. There is no guarantee that mail will be delivered to you, or that any visits will be permitted. The police officer at your side has indicated that you may take a collection of up to 20 personal items with you; the whole collection must fit inside a small suitcase and each item must be a single object - one book, cassette, etc. Your small cell will have a powerpoint and desk, but radios, transmitters, telephones and TV are forbidden. Clothing and food are provided

The police officer indicates that you have only a few minutes to select your items. List them on this page. If time permits, jot down your reasons for taking each one.

1.......	2.......	3.......	4.......
5.......	6.......	7.......	8.......
9.......	10.......	11.......	12.......
13.......	14.......	5.......	16.......
17.......	18.......	19.......	20.......

Discussion questions
- What values does Jesus contrast in Luke 12: 15-21?
- What is the 'rubbish' referred to by Paul in Philippians 3:4-14? Why does he reject things that once gave him considerable status?
- If life is a 'race', what does Paul have to say about its purpose and prize? Read II Timothy 4:1-7.